AMAZING DAIRY-FREE DESSERTS

PENNY WANTUCK EISENBERG

Surris Books
Charlotte, North Carolina

Publisher's Cataloging-in-Publication
(Provided by Quality Books, Inc.)

Eisenberg, Penny Wantuck.
    Amazing dairy-free desserts / Penny Wantuck Eisenberg.
        p. cm.
        Includes index.
        Library of Congress Control Number: 2006903965
        ISBN 978-0-9779617-9-5

        1. Desserts. 2. Milk-free diet--Recipes.
    I. Title.

    TX773.E359 2006   641.8'6
                                       QBI06-600137

All photos except Pecan Toffee Cheezecake and Rice Pudding © Richard Rudisill

All drawings except first 5 Challah drawings © John Sakal

Cover Photos Fudgy Chewy Brownies, page 76, Maple Walnut Ice Creem, page 40 and Hot Fudge Sauce, page 210, Pecan Toffee Cheezecake, page 63

In memory of my father, Ralph Wantuck, who gave us laughter, music, poetry, and so much more. We miss him.

In honor of my father-in-law, Bernie Eisenberg, whose help made it possible for me to pursue my dreams. He was the best baby and pet sitter anyone could hope for. And he loves my food! We love you.

ACKNOWLEDGMENTS

To my petoo, who makes the world go round, thank you for bringing out the best in me, for your encouragement and for your endless and unconditional love. To the light of our lives, Beth and Eric, thank you for all the joy you give us, and for lots of yochs. To my mom, Roslyn Wantuck, thanks for passing on your can-do spirit and enthusiasm, and for sharing your kitchen. To my sister, Karen Wantuck, thank you for all the professional help you've given me over the last ten years, and of course, thank you for your love and support. To my sister, Leslie Weiner, thanks for insights and intimate talks and unending love and support. To my mother-in-law, Ruth Eisenberg, thank you for always being thoughtful, concerned and giving. To my cousin, Debbie Wantuch, thanks for your warmth and constant caring, and for late-night conversations.

To my editor, Carol Wiley Lorente, thank you so much for help in making my writing more concise and descriptive. To Mary Phillips, Maureen Fortune and Ardith Bradshaw at Wimmer Cookbooks, thank you for your finishing touches to the design of the book and for bringing it to life on the printed page. To the many others at Wimmer who contributed to the printing and distribution of the book, many thanks. Thanks to Lisa Ekus for unmatched public relations and for her advice and patience during difficult times. To Richard Rudisill, thank you for your incredible photos and for the enthusiasm you brought to the project. Thank you, John Sakal for the wonderful drawings that help clarify the instructions.

To Ann DelVecchio, your help at the photo shoot was invaluable. Also, thank you for pulling me out of my empty-nest funk with your enthusiasm, and for encouraging me to play golf. To Jackie Stutts, thank you for helping out at the photo shoot also, and more importantly, for your constant love and support over the years. To Lisa Wohl, who also helped with the photo shoot, thank you for teaching me how to be a true friend. To Chris Beloni, thanks for loaning me several of the plates you hand-crafted.

Thank you to my tasters; mah jong friends: Stacy Doline, Nathalie Malter and Sharon Richter, Mandy Blumenthal for her critiques of my chocolate creations, Samantha and Bradley DelVechhio for their opinions on the cupcakes and frosting and danke Fiama and Fabio Pachaidt for the help with the chocolate chocolate chip cookies. To my new friend, Inga Pachaidt, thank you for lots of hugs, laughter, great ideas and perpetual enthusiasm. Thanks to Lenore Cuyler for lunchtime talks and great golf. Lastly, I am indebted to Roberta Massey, who has kept my kitchen clean and tidy for oh-so many years.

CONTENTS

INTRODUCTION

Writing this book has been a great pleasure because, like 50 million other Americans, I too, am lactose intolerant. As a food professional, who must sometimes use dairy, I've had many uncomfortable hours after consuming it. I know the pain and embarrassment of this problem. Although I consume Lactaid® by the bottle, it's not always effective, it's expensive and sometimes inconvenient. Using these recipes, I know that whatever comes out of my kitchen is safe for me to eat. They've been carefully crafted so that you will have dairy-free desserts that are so good, you will have no need for apology. In fact, if you choose to keep it a secret, your family and friends will be unaware that the delectable treats they are eating are dairy-free.

Those of you who are allergic to dairy and could not even resort to popping a pill, will now have desserts for every occasion and for your whole family. School snacks, birthdays and holidays will no longer be a problem. It is imperative that you choose base ingredients that are dairy-free. Check the Ingredient chapter for a list of foods to avoid, and foods to enjoy and where to buy them. Most importantly, read labels before assuming that a product is dairy-free. Kosher certification is a start to finding the right products, but it should not replace careful attention to labels. Join the Food Allergy and Anaphylaxis Network (FAAN) and you can sign up to get e-mail alerts specific to your allergies. It's also a great resource for material on food allergies. You can reach them at: www.foodallergy.org.

For those of you who shun dairy for religious reasons, health, or environmental reasons, all of the recipes will be suitable for you. If you are kosher, be sure to choose base ingredients that are pareve or have a kosher symbol acceptable to you. Check the Ingredient and Kosher Certification chapters for the kosher classification of ingredients used in this book, and look for special instructions for using kosher products.

All of these recipes are original and from scratch and have been crafted with love in my home kitchen, using the appliances that you would have in your own home kitchen. They have not been reduced from commercial recipes, nor have they been collected from friends and family. Each recipe has been tested and re-tested to create the best taste and texture possible. Ingredients must be of the highest quality to assure results that are excellent. For certain dairy substitutes I have listed brand names, because these are the ones that I think taste like dairy and work well in baking. If you cannot find them locally, check the Ingredient section for online sources. It will be worth the effort when you produce exceptional desserts.

I hope you will love these recipes as much as I do. For updates on new products and sources, additions, corrections, new recipes and photos, please visit me online at: www. pennyeisenberg.com. With sweet thoughts, I wish you happy and safe baking.

DAIRY-FREE BASICS

If you are allergic to milk products, it is imperative that you read food labels. Even a kosher symbol is not reliable proof that a food contains no dairy, as kosher certification may lag behind product change. The Food Allergy and Anaphylaxis Network (FAAN) has a credit card-sized laminated card detailing the foods you should avoid. Among the ingredients that you should avoid are:

milk – including fresh, dry, condensed, evaporated, goat's milk, malted milk, cream, sour cream, milk solids, buttermilk, butter, yogurt, etc.
butter, artificial butter and butter flavorings
cheeses and whey
lactose, lactalbumin, lactoferrin, lactulose, lactaglobulin
ammonium, calcium, caramel color, caramel flavoring
casein and caseinates
high protein flour
magnesium
Opta (fat replacer), Simplesse (fat replacer)
margarine, except for non-dairy margarine
whipped topping, except for non-dairy whipped topping
creamer, except for non-dairy creamer
chocolate, except for non-dairy chocolate

Lactose intolerant individuals can eat casein but should avoid all obvious dairy ingredients, as well as the following:

lactose, whey, curds, milk by-products, dry milk solids, and nonfat dry milk powder.

According to the Food Allergy and Anaphylaxis Network (FAAN), the following ingredients are NOT milk products:

calcium lactate & calcium stearoyl lactylate
cocoa butter
cream of coconut
sodium lactate
sodium stearoyl lactylate
cream of tartar
oleoresin
lactic acid (although lactic acid starter might contain dairy)
cream of coconut

KOSHER SYMBOLS

Because those who keep kosher do not eat milk and meat together, kosher products are certified as either meat, dairy, or dairy-free. This certification is indicated by a marking on the package (see symbols, next page). This can be very useful if you are looking for packaged goods that are dairy-free. One should still check the ingredient list, however, because kosher certification may lag behind product changes.

A dairy-free product will have a kosher symbol with no "D" next to it. It may also have the words 'pareve', or 'parve', which means dairy-free. A "P" next to a kosher symbol does not mean pareve (it means kosher for Passover. It may also be pareve, but the "P" will not tell you that). There are many organizations that confer this certification and a manufacturer may choose one of these, if it operates in their locality or they may have a local rabbi perform the certification. A local certification will often simply have a "K" on it (this may be less reliable, as you don't know the standards used by the rabbi doing the certification). If you have any doubts about a product, contact the manufacturer or find another product to use. Remember that if a kosher product gets re-packaged and then sold, it is no longer kosher unless the place doing the re-packaging also has kosher certification (chocolate, for example, is often bought in large blocks, chopped up and repackaged for resale). Each of the certifying agencies has a website where you can sign up for alerts on products that have changed ingredients or that have been marked incorrectly.

On the next page is a list of the certifying organizations for the products I recommend:

Union of Orthodox Jewish Congregations (OU) - ww.ou.org

 Organized Kashrus Laboratories (OK) - www.ok.org

 Kof-K Kosher Supervision (KOF-K) - www.kof-k.com

 Kosher Supervision of America (KSA) - www.ksakosher.com

 Chicago Rabbinical Council (CRC) - www.crcweb.org

 Triangle K (Triangle K) - www.trianglek.org

 Vaad Hakashrus of Denver (Scroll-K) - www.scrollk.com

 Star-K - www.star-k.com

Chocolate

Because the machinery used to make chocolate is often used for both dairy and non-dairy manufacturing, it would need to be cleaned with water, between manufacturing runs, to receive a kosher - pareve certification. This would be disastrous for chocolate production, as water causes chocolate to seize up. Because of this, most non-dairy chocolate is produced on machines that also make dairy chocolate. The labeling states that there might be dairy in the product. I use some chocolate that is kosher-pareve, some that is kosher-DE (dairy equipment) and some that has no certification. Each brand of chocolate has its own flavor undertone, ranging from musky to fruity. Choose the chocolate that suits your taste, fits your budget and is available to you.

Lindt

If you are not kosher and not allergic, Lindt® Swiss Bittersweet Chocolate (also sold as Lindt Surfin, or Lindt Chocolate Gold Bars) is my favorite chocolate to use. It contains about 53% cocoa and is mellow and smooth. The labeling states that it may contain traces of dairy or nuts, which should not bother you if you are lactose intolerant. However, if you are making a dessert that is non-dairy because of allergy or have religious concerns, you might want to use a different chocolate. You can buy Lindt at Lindt stores, some supermarkets or specialty stores and online at:
www.worldwidechocolate.com — (single bars or 5 pack)
www.candywarehouse.com — excellent price on bulk purchases

Chocolate Emporium

My favorite pareve chocolate comes from the Chocolate Emporium. They repackage and remold Blommer chocolate in an allergy-free and kosher environment. Their chocolate chips (I like the regular ones better than the soy-free ones) are sweet, chocolately and quite reasonably priced. Although Blommer pareve chocolate is produced on dairy-equipment it is certified pareve by Star-K. Chocolate Emporium is con-

fident in Blommer's cleaning process. They state: "They run 30,000 lbs of dairy-free product through after cleaning (still under dairy certification). At this point the product is considered pareve. They test for presence of dairy with each run. Blommer's meticulousness in this regard combined with 13 years of relying on their products gives us confidence in their production methods...We have numerous customers who are anaphylactic to dairy and have had great success with our products."
www.choclat.com

enJoylife Foods
They make a very good, certified kosher-pareve, chocolate chip. Because they are mini-chips, they're perfect for delicate cakes where larger chips might fall to the bottom. They also melt beautifully and can be used whenever semisweet chocolate is called for. I would describe the flavor as very sweet and slightly musky. I find them at the health food store, but you can search their website for a store near you, or order them online. They're also offered in bulk at their website: www.enjoylifefoods.com

Chocolate Decadence
They make a semisweet chocolate bar that is sweet and mellow, having 53% cocoa. (Their chocolate chips are delicious, too, but they are more expensive than enJoylife.) The bars are sold online in a variety 4-pack, but in the special instruction section, you can specify that you only want the plain dark chocolate.
www.chocolatedecadence.com

ScharffenBerger
Whenever a slightly bitter or stronger chocolate taste is needed, I always buy ScharffenBerger. All of their larger semisweet bars are certified kosher-pareve, without any trace of dairy. The semisweet chocolate is 62% cocoa, available in a 9.7-ounce bar that is easy to shave into small pieces for melting or in a 2-kg. propack that is cut into 1 ounce chunks. You

can also order ScharffenBerger unsweetened, in 9.7-ounce bars or in a propack (2-kgs. cut into 1 ounce pieces). ScharffenBerger is a great company to work with, answers questions on-line and sells its chocolate from its site and at fine food and specialty cooking stores, such as Sur La Table. www.ScharffenBerger.com

Callebaut

A maker of fine chocolate, Callebaut has so many different chocolates, it's hard to figure out what is what, and they aren't very good about responding to email. You cannot buy the product directly from them online, either, but there are many distributors who sell retail. Callebaut® has excellent flavor, but is not as smooth as some other chocolates. Their chocolate chips are excellent tasting and priced well, but do not melt well for use in recipes that call for melted semisweet chocolate. According to Miss Robens, an on-line allergy store, Barry-Callebaut says that the chips contain no dairy, are made on a separate line but in a plant that also produces dairy chocolate. If you are allergic, you will need to consider this, but if lactose intolerant this will be fine. Callebaut also makes callets (like big chocolate chips) which are kosher – dairy (no dairy in the ingredients), suitable for lactose intolerance but maybe not for allergies. Buy Callebaut at the following sites:
www.missroben.com -– for chocolate chips (repackaged - not for kosher)
www.abcsugarart.com -– for callets in 1.5 and 22 lb. bags (not for kosher)
www.chocosphere.com -– for 11 pound blocks of pareve (kosher certified)

Ghirardelli

Ghirardelli chocolate chips are quite fruity and almost alcoholic if you eat them right from the bag. However, when cooked this taste dissipates and they have wonderful flavor. It can be certified kosher-dairy because it has traces of dairy in it or because it actually contains dairy, so watch carefully if you plan to use Ghirardelli. None of the products are kosher-pareve, however, and may not be suitable for those with allergies.

Hershey's
For unsweetened chocolate, Hershey's® is great. It's kosher, non-dairy and available in the supermarket. (Baker's® chocolate has milk solids in it and is unsuitable.).

Working with Chocolate

Chocolate will melt more evenly if it is shaved or cut into small lumps. To shave chocolate, use a chef's knife. Plant the tip of the knife on a cutting board and then rock it back and forth to shave off the chocolate into 1/16-inch pieces.

Chocolate burns easily and should not be melted over direct heat. Instead, melt chocolate in a bowl placed over hot, but not simmering, water. If the water is simmering, water from condensation may get into the chocolate and cause it to seize into a thick mess. The water should not touch the bottom of the bowl so that the chocolate does not get too hot. Alternatively, chocolate can be melted in a microwave on medium power. Microwave for 30 - 60 seconds until it starts to look shiny. Stir and continue to heat in 15-second increments until completely melted and smooth. Stir after each burst of heat.

When melting chocolate with another ingredient, make sure that it is at the same temperature, or warmer than the chocolate. For melted butter, margarine and other ingredients containing water, use at least 1 tablespoon liquid per 2 ounces chocolate to ensure that the chocolate will not seize (When blending chocolate with oil, you need not without worry of seizure).

Cocoa

Pure unsweetened cocoa is generally dairy-free (don't buy cocoa drink mix, but pure cocoa). Hershey's is certified OU and Droste is certified OK. Droste is Dutch processed cocoa and Hershey's produces both natural and Dutch processed. Use whichever is called for in the recipe or the taste will be different and the leavening may be affected.

Cookies

For crumb crusts and for making phyllo pastries, I use graham crackers, pecan shortbread and kosher tea biscuits. Most graham crackers do not have dairy in the ingredient list but if you need one that is certified kosher-pareve, look for Murray® with an OU certification or for a store brand that is pareve (I use Harris Teeter's Cinnamon Grahams). In a kosher food store or online, you can buy Rokeach® graham crackers, which also carry an OU certification. Shortbread cookies are a little harder to find. I use Keebler® Sandies® which have no dairy in the ingredient list, but are not certified. Kedem® makes a tea biscuit that is certified OU and can be found at kosher food stores. These are a bit leaner than shortbread cookies, so you might need a little more margarine when making crumb crusts.

Coconut Milk

Coconut milk is a non-dairy product suitable for lactose intolerance. It may be processed on dairy equipment, however, and those who are allergic might need a kosher product. If you are allergic or kosher, you can use Goya® coconut milk if it comes from the Dominican Republic (no kosher symbol but okay according to CRC), or Fiesta Brand® with an OK certification. Some brands of coconut milk have preservatives so check the ingredients, if this is important to you.

Cream Cheese Substitutes

The only cream cheese substitute that I like is Tofutti® Better than Cream Cheese. It tastes remarkably like cream cheese and makes a great cheesecake. When you open it up it should look like a creamy cream cheese. If it's dry and curdly looking, it has been frozen and will not work well in your recipes. If using Tofutti for frosting, do not beat it, as it will thin out to sauce consistency as soon as the sugar is added. If gently mixed with sugar it works well and tastes great. Look for it in health food and kosher stores that carry refrigerated items. All Tofutti products are certified kosher-pareve (non-dairy/non-meat).

Cream of Coconut

Cream of coconut is a very thick, sweetened coconut product. It makes great desserts and does not contain any dairy. If you are allergic or kosher, choose Coco Lopez, as it is certified OU to be dairy-free. You can usually find it in either the baking aisle or with the cocktail items. Make sure to stir it well before using it, as the fat rises to the top, leaving behind the sweet coconut liquid.

Cream Substitutes

If a recipe calls for cream, substitute soy creamer or non-dairy creamer. I prefer soy creamer as it is a healthier product and I like the way it tastes. I use Silk® soy creamer, regular, not vanilla flavor. For information on the kosher certification of Silk, please see Milk Substitutes, page 24. As far as non-dairy creamer goes, I like dairy-case Coffeemate® suitable for lactose intolerance but not for allergy, as it contains a dairy derivative. A pareve creamer, made by Coffeerich®, can be found frozen in many supermarkets. I don't like the flavor quite as much as either of the two already mentioned, but it does work in most of the recipes and is great for allergy sufferers.

Eggs

I almost always use eggs at room temperature because warm eggs beat up better and create better emulsification in batters. Put them (left in the shell) into a bowl of warm water for 3 - 5 minutes to bring them to the right temperature without increasing the risk of salmonella contamination.

According to the American Egg Board, the chance of having an egg with salmonella in it is very small – 1 in 20,000 eggs. Most cases of salmonella poisoning are due to eating eggs that were not only infected, but also stored at the wrong temperature. However, they still recommend not eating raw eggs. You must decide whether it is worth the risk to eat eggs that are uncooked or undercooked. Personally, I never eat uncooked eggs and wouldn't dream of serving them to guests. I buy pasteurized eggs (Davidson's®) when I know that I will be making something that will be undercooked. If you cannot find them, use the alternate ingredients listed in the recipe and cook according to these directions:

Simmer 1-inch of water in a skillet. In a shallow metal bowl, whisk the ingredients listed (usually eggs, liquid and sugar or sweetener). Have a rubber scraper, instant read thermometer, a timer, and another large mixer bowl near the stove. Place the shallow bowl into the simmering water. Rapidly stir with the rubber scraper for 30 seconds. Remove the bowl from the simmering water and take the temperature to see if the eggs are at 160 degrees F. If not, heat the egg mixture for 10 seconds more, remove the bowl from the water, dip the thermometer into the boiling water to clean it, and then recheck. Do not exceed 160 degrees or the eggs will be overcooked. Transfer the egg mixture to the large mixer bowl and continue with the recipe. If you do not have an instant thermometer, combine the ingredients in a metal bowl, place on top of a pot of boiling water and beat the mixture with an electric beater for 7 minutes. Transfer the mixture to a cool mixer bowl and beat until cool.

To whip egg whites, bowls and beaters must be clean, dry and grease-free. Any trace of fat, including egg yolk, will prevent the whites from whipping up properly. For extra assurance, wipe the bowl and beaters with a little vinegar.

To whip egg whites to maximum volume, they should be at room temperature. To test for soft peaks, lift up the beaters slowly; if a little peak forms and the tip slumps back over, the eggs are at soft peak.

Stiff peaks stand straight up and stay up. Many recipes call for whites that are beaten "stiff but not dry". Dry whites will not allow your cake to rise properly. You'll know if they are "dry" because they will ball up and look like little bits of Styrofoam when you try to fold them into your batter. If this happens, beat another egg white into the remaining egg whites and then continue to fold these into the batter.

There are three ways to retard the speed at which eggs become dry. They are: adding sugar or cream of tartar to the whites, or whipping the whites in a copper bowl. Add cream of tartar at the beginning of beating, and add sugar when the whites are foamy throughout. If egg whites are whipped in a copper bowl, a chemical reaction takes place between the egg protein and the copper, creating a very stable and supple foam that makes for moist and high-rising cakes and soufflés. Do not use acidic ingredients (including cream of tartar) in a copper bowl as too much copper may dissolve into the food. Because most mixers do not come with a copper bowl, I have not used a copper bowl to prepare any of these recipes.

To prevent overbeating, beat the whites to soft peaks, fold the egg whites from the bottom of the bowl to the top, and then continue to beat to stiff peaks (or for extra care, finish whisking by hand instead).

If the recipe calls for beating eggs or egg yolks until a ribbon forms, lift up the beaters from the pale eggs and let them fall off the beater and back into the eggs. They should fall in a steady stream - a "ribbon", and then should disappear into the eggs. If the eggs fall in droplets or lumps, beat some more.

Flour

I use Pillsbury® all-purpose flour (OU kosher certification) and Swansdown® cake flour (K kosher certification). If you prefer an OU certification, try to find Soft As Silk® cake flour. I generally measure flour by weight to make sure that my recipes always come out the same. I use 130 grams for a cup of all-purpose flour and 135 grams for bread flour. To approximate this without weighing the flour, fluff up the flour in the canister with a spoon and then dip the measuring cup into the canister. Finish by leveling off the cup with a knife. You'll see this method described in the recipes as "fluffed, scooped, and leveled". For cake flour, I measure 100 grams per cup. My instructions call for sifting the cake flour before measuring, because cake flour is so clumpy that it's hard to accurately measure it unless you sift it first. If weighing any kind of flour, it's unnecessary to presift it.

Liqueurs

Liqueurs are generally dairy-free, but some are not kosher or are kosher/dairy. Check labels to be sure the liqueur has no dairy in it. If you are hypersensitive, you might even want to write to the particular producer. To see which are kosher, please see the Kosher Ingredient List, on page 27.

Margarine

I use Fleischmann's® unsalted stick margarine. It's a non-dairy margarine that is readily available, and it works great in baking. Margarine must be at the proper temperature for good baking results. It gets very soft at room temperature, so I usually use it when it is a bit colder than that. When I am going to beat a batter for 5 - 7 minutes, I use the margarine straight from the refrigerator. By the time it is beaten, it will be at exactly the right temperature for adding the other ingredients. For pastry, margarine is also often used straight from the refrigerator or even frozen. When I combine margarine with chocolate, I use margarine at room temperature, or melted so that the chocolate doesn't seize.

Milk Substitutes

I use a dairy-case soymilk in regular (not vanilla or unsweetened) flavor. There are several brands that are acceptable and you should use the one that you find tastiest. It should taste almost like milk and should not be brown or unappealing to the eye. I usually use Silk® because it is the easiest to find and tastes great. The kosher labeling on Silk is Scroll-K-DE. I contacted White Wave to find out why they don't have a pareve rating. Here is their response: "Silk® Soymilk, Silk Soymilk Creamer and Silk Cultured Soy are dairy-free. That means that we do not use any dairy products (including lactose or casein) in any of our products or their ingredients. The kosher symbol DE on the package indicates that these products are processed on dairy equipment. We understand that many of our consumers use Silk products because they are lactose intolerant or dairy allergic. We are committed to providing a product that is 100% dairy-free and have zero tolerance for dairy content in our products. To this end, all shared equipment is sterilized and cleaned after each run of product. Every batch of Silk Soymilk or Silk Cultured Soy is tested for dairy proteins every 15 minutes during the production run to ensure that our product is completely dairy-free." If you are eating dairy-free because of religious reasons, you will have to decide if this is sufficient. If you are looking for a product that is certified kosher-pareve, Eighth Generation is certified OU. There may also be store brands that are excellent and certified dairy-free.

I also use non-dairy creamer occasionally. For rice pudding, for example, which cooks long and reduces, soymilk does not have the best flavor. Non-dairy creamer is a good alternative for someone who is allergic to soy. Rice Dream® is also suitable for those allergic to soy. I prefer dairy-case Rice Dream to the aseptic packaging. It has no dairy in the ingredients, but is certified kosher-dairy. The aseptic version is pareve.

Sour Cream Substitutes

I've only found one brand of sour cream substitute that I find excellent. Tofutti® Better Than Sour Cream has a taste and texture that is very similar to sour cream and works well in baking. All Tofutti products are certified kosher-pareve (no dairy). Look for Tofutti products in kosher food stores and health food markets. There are several sour cream substitutes on the market that are perfectly awful. If it doesn't taste like sour cream, don't use it in your baking!

Vanilla

Vanilla is an essential flavoring for baked goods. If you use poor quality vanilla, or artificial vanilla, you will not have good flavor in your baked goods. Vanillas have different flavors depending on where they come from. My favorite is Mexican vanilla. I use it when vanilla will be the main flavor and I want it to really shine. Custards and pound cakes, for example, taste really special with Mexican vanilla. For foods in which vanilla is not the main flavor, such as chocolate or coffee-flavored desserts, I often use Madagascar Bourbon vanilla. It has a very nice taste that combines well with other flavors. I have tried Tahitian vanilla and it has a unique, almost flowery, taste. You will have to try it and see if it suits your taste. To me, it doesn't taste like vanilla and I don't use it if I want a vanilla taste. My favorite brand of vanilla is Niellsen-Massey®.

Whipped Cream Substitutes

You might be surprised to know that most whipped toppings that you find in the supermarket contain dairy. In addition, they are very marshmallowy and do not taste like whipped cream. The very best whipped cream substitute that I've ever tasted is Richwhip®. It comes as a frozen liquid in an eight-ounce carton. Defrost it and then whip it just as if it were whipping cream. It can be whipped to mounds, soft or stiff peaks. It also "weeps" or waters out if it stands, just like whipped cream, and can be stabilized exactly like whipped cream. Make sure that the stabilizer you use does not contain dairy (I use Oetker Whipit®, which has no dairy in the ingredients). Richwhip also comes pre-whipped, but I don't use it because I prefer the taste and texture of the Richwhip I prepare myself. Richwhip is available in some supermarkets and at kosher food stores. Richwhip is compiling a list of retail stores that sell their products. It will eventually be posted on their website at: www.whiptopping.com. In the meantime contact The Kosher Mart and Deli at: www.koshermartusa.com; they will be happy to ship you some overnight.

KOSHER LIST

Chocolate
enjoylifefoods semisweet chocolate chips – CRC, pareve
Lindt Semisweet Chocolate – uncertified (no dairy in ingredients)
Chocolate Decadence Dark Chocolate Bars – certified non-dairy by Rabbi Yonah H. Gellar
ScharffenBerger Semisweet Bars (9.7 ounce bars and larger) - KSA, pareve, (smaller bars) - KSA, DE
Callebaut – varies – Semisweet 811 callets-K-Dairy (no dairy in ingredients),
Ghirardelli Semisweet Bars- KOF-K, D (some products have dairy in ingredients; some do not)
Hershey's Unsweetened – OU

Cocoa
Hershey's – OU
Droste – OK

Coconut Milk
Goya (from Dominican Republic only)
Fiesta – OK

Coconut – Sweetened
Baker's Sweetened Coconut - OK

Cookies
Murray's Grahams – OU, pareve
Hannaford Grahams – OU, pareve
Rokeach Grahams – OU, pareve
Keebler Sandies – uncertified (no dairy in ingredients)
Kedem Tea Biscuits – OU, parve

Cream Cheese Substitute
Tofutti Better Than Cream Cheese – KOF-K, parve

Cream of Coconut
Coco Lopez – OU

Creamers
Silk – Scroll-K, DE (see explanation page 24)
Coffeemate – OU, D (contains casein, so is okay for lactose intolerance)
CoffeeRich – OU, pareve

Flour
Pillsbury – OU
Swansdown – K
Soft As Silk – OU

Dried and Canned Fruit
Sunmaid Raisins- TRIANGLE K
Del Monte Canned Pineapple- TRIANGLE K

Gelatin
Knox – unsupervised (a non-dairy meat product)
KoJel Unsweetened Gelee – OU, parve

Liqueurs
Godiva (kosher, no symbol)
Amaretto di Saronno - OU
Frangelico – kosher if it bears an OU
Drambuie (kosher, no symbol)
Curacao (kosher, no symbol)
Godiva Chocolate - OU
Melody Banana or Triple Sec - OU
Sabra Chocolate Orange, or Coffee - OU
Rum – any unflavored, except Don Quixote - kosher, no symbol
Kahlúa, Kirsch, Tia Maria, Cointreau, Galliano and Grand Marnier are not kosher

Margarine and Shortening
Fleischmann's Unsalted Stick – OU, pareve
Crisco – OU

Marshmallow Fluff
OU, pareve

Phyllo
Athens – OK, pareve

Sour Cream Substitutes
Tofutti Better Than Sour Cream – KOF-K, parve

Soymilk
Silk – Scroll-K, DE (see explanation page 24)
Eighth Generation – OU

Vanilla
Nielsen-Massey – CRC

Whipped Cream Substitute
Richwhip – OU, pareve

ICE CREEM, PUDDINGS, ETC.

Chocolate Ice Creem

MAKES 5 CUPS

Unlike dairy-free ice cream substitutes that you find in the market, this
one tastes just like the real thing, with
no off tastes or oily texture. Made
with a bold, semisweet chocolate,
it's rich, smooth and deeply satisfy-
ing. If you haven't made ice cream
in recent years, you'll find the new
electric ice cream makers easy and
fun to use.

1/3 cup dairy-case Silk® soy creamer or non-
dairy creamer
3 ounces bold semisweet chocolate, (such
as ScharffenBerger®), cut into small chunks
2 large pasteurized eggs, room temperature
(for regular eggs, see sidebar, next page)
1 large pasteurized egg yolk, room
temperature
1/3 cup sugar
1 tablespoon corn syrup
1/4 teaspoon vanilla extract
1-1/4 cups Richwhip®, thawed

1. Place the creamer in a medium-size microwave-safe container. Microwave on
high, for 30 seconds. Add the chocolate
and let it rest a minute. Stir, and if not
melted, heat on medium, in 15-second
increments, until the chocolate is melted.
Set aside to cool.

2. In a large mixer bowl, using a balloon
whisk attachment, beat together the eggs
and egg yolk. Beat in the sugar, corn
syrup and vanilla. Continue to beat on
high, until the egg mixture triples in volume (about 5 - 7 minutes). On low speed,
beat in the cooled chocolate mixture.

For pasteurized eggs, look for Davidson's® eggs, in the shell.

*If using regular eggs, melt the chocolate with 3 tablespoons of creamer. In a shallow metal bowl, mix together the egg, yolk, sugar, corn syrup and the remaining creamer. Simmer 1-inch of water in a skillet. Have a rubber scraper, instant-read thermometer, a timer and a large mixer bowl near the stove. Place the shallow bowl into the simmering water and cook the egg mixture to 160 degrees F. (30 – 60 seconds), rapidly stirring with a rubber scraper and checking the temperature every 15 seconds. Transfer the mixture to a large mixer bowl and continue with the recipe.

3. Pour the Richwhip® into a small mixer bowl. Beat on high speed, until the Richwhip® forms soft peaks (or just until mounding if you prefer ice cream that freezes harder). Fold into the chocolate mixture.

4. Transfer the mixture to an ice cream machine (I use an inexpensive Cuisinart® ice cream maker) and process according to manufacturer's instructions. (It's okay if the mixture fills the freezing container completely because it will deflate as it is churned, not inflate the way regular ice cream does). After 30 minutes, if your machine has a removable freezer container, remove the dasher and place the container of ice cream into the freezer. Giving it a few folds every fifteen minutes, freeze the ice creem for another hour until it starts to firm up and look like regular ice cream. Transfer the ice cream to a storage container and continue to freeze for several hours until it is the texture you like.

VARIATIONS

Chocolate Nut – add 3/4 cup nuts during the last 5 minutes of churning.

Chocolate Chocolate Flake – add chocolate flakes, see Macadamia Chocolate Flake Ice Creem, page 38

Chocolate Brownie – add 1-1/2 to 2 Fudgy Chewy Brownies, page 76, cut into 1/4-inch squares.

Toasted Almond
Ice Creem

MAKES 4 CUPS

2 eight-ounce containers Richwhip®, thawed
3 tablespoons sugar
1 tablespoon corn syrup
2 tablespoons amaretto liqueur (for kosher,
use Amaretto di Saronno®)
1/2 cup Silk® soy creamer or non-dairy
creamer
1/8 teaspoon vanilla extract
1/8 teaspoon almond extract
1/2 cup slivered almonds, toasted in a
toaster-oven for 2 - 3 minutes until barely
browning, lightly crushed

This delicately flavored ice cream, made without eggs, is perfect for vegans and those watching cholesterol. It's very rich and slightly more icy than ice creem made with eggs. If you prefer it, you can adapt all of the ice cream recipes to this method.

1. Combine all ingredients, except the almonds, in a large mixer bowl. Beat on high speed until the mixture is just starting to mound.

2. Transfer the mixture to an ice cream maker (I use an inexpensive Cuisinart® ice cream maker) and process according to manufacturer's instructions. (It's okay if the mixture fills the freezing container completely because it will deflate as it is churned, not inflate the way regular ice cream does). After 30 minutes, churn in the almonds. If your machine has a removable freezer container, remove the dasher

and place the container of ice creem into the freezer. Giving it a few folds every 15 minutes, freeze the ice creem for another hour, until it starts to firm up and look like regular ice cream. Transfer the ice creem to a storage container and continue to freeze it for several hours until it is the texture you like.

Vanilla Ice Creem

One standard way of making vanilla ice cream is to chill and freeze a rich custard. This method does not work well with non-dairy ingredients, so I've created a method that's easier and makes a very creamy ice creem. Adjust the amount of sugar and vanilla to get the taste that is perfect for you.

MAKES 5 CUPS

3 large pasteurized eggs (for regular eggs, see sidebar, next page)
1-inch piece vanilla bean, split lengthwise with one end still attached
1/4 cup sugar
1 tablespoon corn syrup
1/3 cup Silk® soy creamer or non-dairy creamer
1-1/4 cups Richwhip®, thawed

1. Put the eggs (in the shell) into a bowl of hot water for 10 minutes (this will heat the eggs to warmer than room temperature). Break two of the eggs into a large mixer bowl. Separate the remaining egg, discard the white and add the yolk to the bowl. Whisk in the vanilla bean, sugar and corn syrup. With a balloon whisk attachment, on medium-high, beat the egg mixture until it triples in volume, and comes to room temperature (about 5 - 7 minutes). Remove the vanilla bean, and scrape the seeds into the egg mixture. Beat in the creamer.

2. Pour the Richwhip® into a small mixer bowl. Beat on high speed until the Richwhip® forms soft peaks (or just until mounding if you prefer ice cream that freezes harder). Fold into the egg mixture.

For pasteurized eggs, look for David-son's® eggs, in the shell.

If using regular eggs, mix together the eggs, egg yolk, vanilla bean, sugar, corn syrup, and 3 tablespoons of the creamer in a shallow metal bowl (reserve the remaining creamer to add in later). Simmer 1-inch of water in a skillet. Have a rubber scraper, instant-read thermometer, a timer and a large mixer bowl near the stove. Place the shallow bowl into the simmering water and cook the egg mixture to 160 degrees F. (30 – 60 seconds), rapidly stirring with a rubber scraper and checking the temperature every 15 seconds. Transfer the mixture to a large mixer bowl and continue with the recipe.

3. Transfer the mixture to an ice cream maker (I use an inexpensive Cuisinart® ice creem maker) and process according to manufacturer's instructions. (It's okay if the mixture fills the freezing container completely because it will deflate as it is churned, not inflate the way regular ice cream does). After 30 minutes, if your machine has a removable freezer container, remove the dasher and place the container of ice creem into the freezer. Giving it a few folds every fifteen minutes, freeze the ice creem for another hour until it starts to firm up and look like regular ice cream. Transfer the ice creem to a storage container and continue to freeze for several hours until it is the texture you like.

VARIATIONS
Vanilla Brownie Ice Creem
Cut up 2 or 3 Fudgy Chewy Brownies (page 76) into 1/2-inch cubes. Gently fold them into the ice creem after it has churned and is still soft. Freeze several hours until firm enough to scoop.

If you're feeling deprived, this ice creem will make your spirits soar. For the chocolate flakes or chunks use a full-bodied chocolate, such as ScharffenBerger®, because chocolate tends to lose flavor when frozen. Oil is added to the chocolate to give it a nice mouthfeel when it's frozen. You can add more oil if you want the chunks even softer, or use less oil if you want the chunks harder.

Macadamia Chocolate Flake Ice Creem

MAKES 5 CUPS

1 ounce semisweet non-dairy chocolate, chopped

1/2 teaspoon vegetable oil

2 large pasteurized eggs, room temperature (for regular eggs, see sidebar, next page)

1 large pasteurized egg yolk, room temperature

1/4 cup packed light brown sugar

1/8 teaspoon vanilla extract

1/3 cup Silk® soy creamer or non-dairy creamer

1-1/4 cups Richwhip®, thawed

1/2 cup dry roasted, salted macadamia nuts, chopped medium-fine

1. Place the chocolate and oil in a microwave-safe bowl. Microwave on medium for 1 minute. Stir, and then microwave in 15-second increments, until the chocolate is melted and smooth. Place a piece of waxed paper on a plate. Pour the chocolate onto the waxed paper and spread it to a 1/16-inch thick layer, or slightly thicker. Freeze the chocolate until firm. Dice it into small chunks and then refrigerate until ready to use.

For pasteurized eggs, look for David-son's® eggs, in the shell.

If using regular eggs, mix together the eggs, brown sugar and 2 table-spoons creamer, in a shallow metal bowl. Simmer 1-inch of water in a skillet. Have a rubber scraper, in-stant-read thermometer, a timer and a large mixer bowl near the stove. Place the shallow bowl into the sim-mering water and cook the egg mixture to 160 degrees F. (30 – 60 seconds), rapidly stirring with a rub-ber scraper and checking the tem-perature every 15 seconds. Transfer the mixture to a large mixer bowl and continue with the recipe, adding the remaining creamer at the appropri-ate time.

2. In a large mixer bowl, with a balloon whisk attachment, beat together the eggs and egg yolk. On low speed, beat in the brown sugar and vanilla.

3. Increase the speed to medium-high and continue to beat until the egg mixture is very thick and billowy (about 5 - 7 min-utes). Reduce the speed to low and beat in the creamer.

4. Pour the Richwhip® into a small mixer bowl. Beat on high speed until the Rich-whip® just barely forms soft peaks (or just until mounding if you prefer ice cream that freezes harder). Fold into the egg mixture.

5. Transfer the mixture to an ice cream maker (I use an inexpensive Cuisinart® ice creem maker) and process according to manufacturer's instructions. (It's okay if the mixture fills the freezing container completely because it will deflate as it is churned, not inflate the way regular ice cream does). After 30 minutes churn in the nuts and the chocolate flakes. If your machine has a removable freezer contain-er, remove the dasher and place the con-tainer of ice creem into the freezer. Giving it a few folds every fifteen minutes, freeze the ice creem for another hour until it starts to firm up and look like regular ice cream. Transfer the ice creem to a storage container and continue to freeze it for sev-eral hours until it is the texture you like.

Maple Walnut
Ice Creem

MAKES 1 QUART

This ice creem has a bold flavor and a dense, creamy texture. Best served the day it's made, it's fabulous alone or on a brownie with hot fudge sauce.

2 large pasteurized eggs, room temperature (*for regular eggs, see next page)
1 large pasteurized egg yolk, room temperature
1/4 cup pure maple syrup
1/2 cup Silk® soy creamer or non-dairy creamer
1 eight-ounce container Richwhip®, thawed
1/2 cup walnuts, chopped medium-fine

1. In a large mixer bowl, beat together the eggs and egg yolk. Beat in the maple syrup for 5 - 7 minutes until the egg mixture is thick and fluffy. Reduce the speed to low and beat in the creamer.

2. Pour the Richwhip® into a small mixer bowl. Beat on high speed until the Richwhip® just barely forms soft peaks (or just until mounding if you prefer ice cream that freezes harder). Fold into the egg mixture.

3. Transfer the mixture to an ice cream maker and process according to manufacturer's instructions. After 30 minutes, churn in the walnuts. If your machine has a removable freezer container, remove the dasher and place the container

If using regular eggs, whisk together the eggs, egg yolks, maple syrup and 2 tablespoons creamer. Simmer 1-inch of water in a skillet. Have a rubber scraper, instant-read thermometer, a timer and a large mixer bowl near the stove. Place the shallow bowl into the simmering water and cook the egg mixture to 160 degrees F. (30 – 60 seconds), rapidly stirring with a rubber scraper and checking the temperature every 15 seconds. Transfer the mixture to a large mixer bowl and continue with the recipe.

of ice creem into the freezer. Giving it a few folds every 15 minutes, freeze the ice creem for another hour until it starts to firm up and look like regular ice cream. Transfer the ice cream to a storage container and continue to freeze for several hours until it is the texture you like.

Pistachio Ice Creem

This ice creem has a natural pista-chio flavor and a tan color, rather than the garish green that is associ-ated with commercial ice cream. If you need the green color to define the pistachio taste, add some green food coloring. The ice creem stands alone, but is also great in profiteroles or in a bowl with hot fudge.

MAKES 5 CUPS
STEEP PISTACHIOS 1 NIGHT AHEAD

1-3/4 cups shelled, white pistachios (salted or unsalted)

2 cups boiling water

1 cup Silk® soy creamer or non-dairy creamer

2 large pasteurized eggs (for regular eggs, see sidebar, next page)

3 tablespoons sugar

1 tablespoon corn syrup

1/4 teaspoon vanilla extract

1 eight-ounce container Richwhip®, thawed

1. Preheat the oven to 300 degrees F. Place the pistachios in a small bowl, and pour the boiling water over them. Let sit for a minute and then drain. Turn the pista-chios out onto a clean kitchen towel, fold part of the towel over the nuts and rub back and forth to remove the skins from the pistachios. Pour the nuts into a bak-ing pan. Place in the oven for 10 minutes to dry them. Remove any dark brown nuts.

2. Chop 3/4 cup pistachios and set aside. Transfer the remaining pistachios to a food processor. Pour in the creamer and process until the nuts are finely ground.

Tips

*For regular eggs, in a shallow metal bowl, whisk together the eggs, 2 tablespoons of the creamer (the remainder gets added, as per recipe), sugar and corn syrup. Simmer 1-inch of water in a skillet. Have a rubber scraper, instant-read thermometer, a timer and a large mixer bowl near the stove. Place the shallow bowl into the simmering water and cook the egg mixture to 160 degrees F. (30 – 60 seconds), rapidly stirring with a rubber scraper and checking the temperature every 15 seconds. Transfer the mixture to a large mixer bowl and continue with the recipe.

Transfer the mixture to a storage container, cover and refrigerate overnight.

3. When ready to make the ice cream, strain the pistachio-creamer, reserving 3/4 cup of liquid. Refrigerate until ready to use. Discard any remaining liquid and the solids.

4. Place the eggs (in the shell) into a bowl of warm water, to cover, and let them warm up for 10 minutes (they'll get warmer than room temperature). Break the eggs into a large mixer bowl. Whisk in the sugar, corn syrup and vanilla extract.

5. Using a balloon whisk attachment (if available), beat the egg mixture on medium-high until it triples in volume and is thick and billowy (about 5 - 7 minutes). On low, beat in the pistachio-creamer.

6. Place the Richwhip® in a small mixer bowl. Beat on high speed until the Richwhip® forms soft peaks (or just until mounding if you prefer ice cream that freezes harder). Fold into the egg mixture.

7. Transfer the mixture to an ice cream machine and freeze as per previous ice creem recipes, stirring in the reserved pistachios after 30 minutes.

Bananas Foster

SERVES 4 - 6

I like Bananas Foster sweet, with a mild banana flavor and easy on the alcohol. To achieve this, I lightly sauté the bananas first and then set them aside. The liquor is added directly to the sauce and mellows as it cooks. It's quick and simple to prepare and can be altered to get exactly the taste that suits you. If you opt to flame the dish, be very careful, tie back loose hair and clothes and don't flame underneath your cabinets!

5 tablespoons unsalted non-dairy stick margarine (such as Fleischmann's®), room temperature, divided
3 large bananas, peeled and sliced lengthwise and then in half, crosswise
1/2 cup packed light brown sugar
1/4 teaspoon cinnamon
Pinch nutmeg
1/2 cup banana liqueur (*for kosher, see next page)
1/4 cup rum
1 recipe Vanilla Ice Creem, page 36

1. In a large skillet, over high heat, melt 1 tablespoon of margarine until it sizzles. Quickly sauté the bananas, flat side down, just until lightly browned (about 1 minute). Set aside.

2. Melt the remaining margarine in the skillet over medium-low heat. Add the brown sugar and stir until melted (about 2 minutes). Stir in the cinnamon and nutmeg. For a very mellow taste, add the banana liqueur and the rum. Simmer for about 5 minutes, stirring constantly. Turn off the heat. Using a flat whisk, vigorously whisk to incorporate the margarine. Stir in the bananas. Serve the sauce and bananas over Vanilla Ice Creem, page 36.

The sauce may be made ahead and stored in the refrigerator for a week. When ready to serve, sauté the bananas, remove them from the pan, heat up the sauce and continue with the recipe.

*for kosher liqueur, use Melody® banana liqueur, or substitute an orange-flavored liqueur, such as Drambuie®, Curacao®, etc.

3. If you like a more pronounced alcohol taste, reserve the rum. After the sauce has cooked for 5 minutes, heat the rum in a small saucepan. Flame it with a long match and pour it into the sauce. When the flames subside, add the bananas, spoon the sauce over them and then serve. If you want to flame, but don't want too much alcohol taste, add half the rum to the sauce in the beginning, and then flame the remaining rum. For more banana flavor, leave the bananas in the sauce longer and they will continue to soften and become more flavorful.

Eggless, deli-style rice pudding may be the smoothest and creamiest rice pudding you've ever tasted. For a richer taste, increase the proportion of creamer to water. Both sushi rice and Arborio rice are excellent for rice pudding as neither gets hard upon refrigeration. I prefer sushi rice to Arborio because it bubbles up less, and is therefore easier to cook.

Rice Pudding Deli-Style

SERVES 6 - 8

1 cup Japanese sushi or Arborio rice
6 cups water, divided
1-1/2-inch piece vanilla bean, split
  lengthwise with one end still attached
1/4 teaspoon salt
1-1/2 cups non-dairy creamer, divided
  (do not use soymilk)
2/3 cup sugar
3/4 cup raisins
Cinnamon and nutmeg to taste

1. Place the rice, 2 cups water, vanilla bean and salt in a 3-quart pot. Bring it to a boil over high heat. Cover, reduce the heat and simmer for 20 minutes.

2. Meanwhile, place 1-1/4 cups creamer, remaining water and sugar in another 3-quart pot, and bring to a boil over medium-high heat. Cover, reduce the heat to low and keep warm until the rice is done cooking.

3. Remove the vanilla bean, scrape the vanilla seeds into the creamer mixture and then drop the vanilla pod back into the mixture. Ladle the creamer mixture into the cooked rice, stirring gently to break up any lumps. Place the pot over me-

Tips

Rice pudding keeps for 1 week in the refrigerator.

Do not freeze.

dium-high heat and bring to a simmer. Simmer uncovered, for about 30 minutes, stirring occasionally. Stir in the raisins (If they are not soft and plump to begin with, add them about five 5 minutes earlier). The pudding will be thickened, but still soupy. Spoon the pudding into a 9 x 12-inch decorative glass baking dish. Press a piece of nonstick aluminum foil (nonstick side down) directly onto the rice pudding, leaving the edges loose so that excess steam can escape. Let the pudding cool briefly and then refrigerate until completely cool (about 6 hours).

4. The pudding may look unappealing when you uncover it. Don't worry! Mix in enough of the reserved creamer to create a firm pudding with just a bit of creamy sauce, or to get the texture you prefer. Grate some fresh nutmeg over the pudding and lightly sprinkle it with cinnamon. The pudding will now look yummy! For a more decorative service, spoon the pudding into individual goblets or bowls and sprinkle each serving with nutmeg and cinnamon.

Unlike traditional bread pudding, this version doesn't need to be baked in a water-bath. Dairy-free bread is often hard to find, so I make my own (recipe follows). Challah has a tender, eggy crust, which gives the rice pudding a nice taste and texture. The accompanying sauce is a standard custard sauce, but when made without dairy it needs a little cornstarch and powdered sugar to give it some body.

Bread Pudding with Rum Custard Sauce

SERVES 6 - 9

8 ounces non-dairy bread, cubed to make 6 cups (see Challah, page 51)

4 large eggs
1/3 cup plus 1 tablespoon sugar
1 teaspoon vanilla extract
1 teaspoon cinnamon
1/4 teaspoon freshly grated nutmeg
1-1/4 cups dairy-case soymilk (such as Silk®)
1-1/4 cups Silk® soy creamer, or non-dairy creamer

1/3 cup raisins

Rum Custard Sauce (Crème Anglaise)
1/4 cup powdered sugar
4 large egg yolks
1/4 teaspoon cornstarch
1/2 cup plus 1 tablespoon Silk® soy creamer, or non-dairy creamer
1/2 cup dairy-case soymilk (such as Silk®)
2-inch piece vanilla bean, split lengthwise, with one end still attached
1 tablespoon rum

1. Preheat the oven to 325 degrees F. with a rack in the lower third of the oven. Grease an 8 x 8-inch square glass baking dish.

Tips

Custard tends to form a skin over the top as it cools so it is customary to press a covering directly onto the top of it to prevent this. Choices include plastic wrap, foil or a thin film of oil or melted margarine. With plastic wrap, a lot of the custard will stick to it, and chemicals may leach out of it into the custard. Melted margarine hardens on top of the custard, making it difficult to both remove it or stir it in. Oil works, but then you have added an ingredient that you don't particularly want in your sauce. Non-stick foil, my first choice, works well because it doesn't stick to the custard and is easy to remove. However, you shouldn't use foil with acidic ingredients, such as lemon curd, as it will react with the food.

2. Place the bread cubes on a baking sheet and lightly toast in the oven for 5 minutes (they should not brown, but should become somewhat dry.) Let cool (If the bread is already stale, it doesn't need to be toasted)

3. In a medium bowl, lightly whisk the eggs, sugar, vanilla, cinnamon, nutmeg, soymilk and creamer. Stir in the bread and raisins. Turn the mixture into the prepared pan. Let the bread soak in the soymilk mixture for 15 minutes, pressing occasionally with the back of a spoon. Submerge the raisins, as they get too hard if baked exposed. **Bake 60 - 70 minutes** until a knife inserted into the center comes out clean. Cool the pudding on a wire rack for at least 1 hour. If you prefer a firmer pudding, refrigerate it until near serving time and then microwave the pudding just until barely warm.

4. For the sauce: In a medium size bowl, lightly whisk together the powdered sugar, egg yolks and cornstarch.

5. Place the creamer, soymilk and vanilla bean in a medium pot. Add the rum now, if you want to burn off some of the alcohol. For a more alcoholic taste, add the rum when the soymilk mixture is removed from the heat. Place the soymilk mixture over medium heat, and bring it to a simmer.

Tips

Bread pudding can be made 2 days ahead and stored in the refrigerator. Just before serving, microwave it until warmed through.

The sauce can be served cold, room temperature or warm. To re-warm the custard, place it in the top of a double boiler and heat over simmering water. It can also be reheated in the microwave, on low power.

6. Drop by drop, whisk the soymilk mixture into the egg yolk mixture. As the eggs warm up, the soymilk mixture can be added faster and faster. When half of the soymilk mixture has been added, transfer everything back into the pot. Cook on medium heat, until bubbles appear around the edges of the pot and the mixture coats the back of a wooden spoon.

7. Strain the custard into a storage container. Remove the vanilla bean, scrape the vanilla seeds into the custard and then add the pod back into the sauce. Press a piece of nonstick aluminum foil down onto the surface of the custard (Never use foil with acidic ingredients). Let cool briefly and then refrigerate. When the custard is cold, cover it firmly.

VARIATIONS

Add or substitute other dried fruits, such as cherries, dates, diced apples or pears, or add chocolate chips or coconut.

Challah

MAKES 1 LOAF

2/3 cup warm water
2 tablespoons honey
2 tablespoons oil
3/4 teaspoon salt
1 large egg, room temperature

3 cups bread flour, fluffed, scooped and
   leveled into measuring cups
1-1/2 teaspoons rapid-rise, quick-rising or
   instant yeast

1 large egg, for glazing
Poppy seeds, for sprinkling

This braided Jewish sweet bread makes wonderful bread pudding and great French toast. It can be made in a bread machine or with a mixer but is best baked in the oven, so it can develop its distinguishing crust. If I'm making a challah specifically for bread pudding or French toast, I do a simple 3-strand braid rather than the traditional 6-strand braid. Braiding contributes to both taste and texture and is an essential characteristic of Challah.

1. To make the bread in a bread machine, place the water, honey, oil, salt and egg in the bread machine bowl, in the order listed. Add the flour and yeast. Use the dough cycle. After the dough has doubled (about 1 hour), proceed with the shaping instructions.

2. To make the bread in a mixer, place the water, honey, oil, salt, egg, 2-3/4 cups flour, and the yeast in the mixer bowl. Mix on low speed, with a flat beater attachment, until the dough starts to clump together. Switch to the dough hook and knead on medium-low speed, adding the remaining 1/4 cup flour, if needed, to keep the dough from sticking. Continue kneading for 8 - 12 minutes. The dough should be moist and supple but not overly sticky. Transfer the dough to an oiled

Tips

To test if the dough has doubled, flour a finger and gently poke the dough. If the indentation remains, the dough has risen sufficiently.

bowl. Turn the dough over in the bowl so that all sides are oiled. Cover with plastic wrap and leave at room temperature to rise until doubled in volume (about 1 hour). Turn the dough out onto a work surface. Divide the dough into three equal pieces. Form each piece into a rope (it's easier to roll the pieces if the work surface has not been floured). Braid the pieces together. Place the bread on a baking sheet that has been greased and sprinkled with de-germinated cornmeal or flour. Cover the bread with a cotton dish towel and let it rise until doubled (about 30 - 45 minutes). To see if the dough has doubled, flour a finger and gently poke the dough. It should spring back. Be careful not to poke too hard, as you don't want to deflate the dough.

3. Preheat the oven to 375 degrees F. with a rack in the middle of the oven. Mix the egg with 1 teaspoon water to make a glaze. Brush the glaze over the bread and sprinkle with poppy seeds.

4. Set the dough into the middle of the oven and **bake 5 minutes**. Reduce the temperature to 350 degrees F. Brush the bread again with the glaze and continue to **bake 15 - 20 minutes** more, until the bread sounds hollow when tapped on the bottom (the internal temperature should be 190 - 200 degrees F.). Place the bread on a cooling rack. Do not cut the bread until completely cooled.

If you'd like to make a 6-strand braid, double the recipe and make it in a mixer. Divide the dough into 6 equal pieces and form each into a 12-inch rope. Attach the ropes at one end.

Tips

A completed six-strand challah

Braid as follows:

1. Move strand #2 past #6. Renumber the strands, left to right.

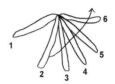

2. Move strand #1 between #3 and #4. Renumber the strands.

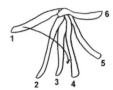

3. Move #5 up to the #1 position. Re-number the strands.

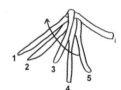

4. Move #6 between #3 and #4.

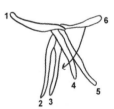

5. Begin the sequence again, moving the strands in the order you have just completed: 2-1-5-6, until the whole bread is braided.

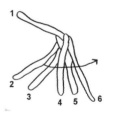

Crème Caramel (Flan)

SERVES 6
MAKE 1 DAY AHEAD

3/4 cup sugar
1/2 cup water

Flan:
4 large eggs, room temperature
2 large egg yolks, room temperature
1/2 cup sugar
1 cup dairy-case soymilk (such as Silk®)
1 cup Silk® soy creamer or non-dairy
   creamer
2-inch piece vanilla bean split lengthwise or
   1-1/2 teaspoons vanilla extract

1. Preheat the oven to 325 degrees F. Boil water for a Bain-Marie (water bath). Place six 6-ounce ramekins (custard cups) in a roasting pan.

2. Place 3/4 cup sugar and water in a small, shiny pot (shiny, so that you can see when the caramel is the right color). Cook, on medium heat, stirring occasionally until the sugar melts. Increase the heat to bring the mixture to a simmer. When the syrup starts to simmer, stop stirring and continue to cook, swirling occasionally, until the color begins to turn golden (about

Whether called Crème Caramel (Renversée) or Flan, this vanilla-flavored custard has a caramel outer edge and a luscious caramel sauce that spills out when the custard is turned upside down onto a serving plate. Be sure to make it at least a day in advance so that the custard can chill and the caramel can soften.

To get the flan out of the ramekins, run a knife along the inside edge of each ramekin to loosen it. Set the ramekins in a roaster with a little boiling water in the bottom for 10 - 15 seconds. Place a plate on the top of each ramekin and then invert. Not all of the caramel will come out of each ramekin, but there should be plenty of sauce for each (the caramel liquefies continually, so there will be more sauce with each progressive day that it is refrigerated). Flan is delicious garnished with fresh berries, bananas, whipped topping or a scoop of ice creem. Cookies are also a nice accompaniment.

Flan may be stored in the refrigerator for up to 1 week. Do not freeze.

12 - 15 minutes). Reduce the heat to low and continue cooking and swirling constantly, until the color is medium-brown and the mixture smells like caramel. Divide the caramel evenly among the ramekins. Swirl the ramekins to coat the bottoms and 1/4-inch up the sides.

3. In a large bowl, lightly whisk together the eggs, yolks and sugar.

4. Combine the soymilk, creamer and vanilla bean in a small pot (if using extract, add it after the mixture is removed from the heat). Heat over medium heat until steam rises from the pot, and the mixture is just about to simmer. Whisk the soymilk mixture into the egg mixture, drop by drop, adding more and more soymilk as the mixture warms up. Strain the mixture into a measuring cup. Scrape the vanilla seeds out of the pod and add to the custard. Pour the custard into the ramekins.

5. Pour boiling water into the roasting pan until it comes halfway up the ramekin sides. **Bake for 25 - 35 minutes** or until a skewer inserted into the custard, 1/8-inch from the edge, comes out clean, but the center still quivers. Remove the ramekins from the Bain Marie and set aside to cool for about 1 hour. Cover each with plastic wrap and refrigerate overnight or up to 4 days.

Chocolate Fondue

SERVES 6 - 8

Chocolate fondue will only be as good as the chocolate you use, so use the very best chocolate that you can find. It's very easy to make and sheer heaven to eat. It couldn't hurt to add a little ice creem on the side!

1/3 to 1/2 cup Silk® soy creamer or non-dairy creamer
2 tablespoons sugar
1 tablespoon liqueur of choice (hazelnut, amaretto, or Drambuie® are excellent. See page 28, for kosher liqueurs)
8 ounces non-dairy semisweet chocolate, finely chopped, (see pages 15-18, for brands)

4 small bananas, cut into 3/4-inch chunks
3 to 4 pieces of each, per person: strawberries, pineapple chunks, non-dairy 1-inch cubes of poundcake (see page 117), halved or mini-marshmallows, etc.

1. Simmer 1-1/2 inches water in the bottom of a double boiler and then reduce the heat to just keep the water warm. Place 1/3 cup creamer and the sugar in the top of the double boiler. Place directly over a medium burner and cook, stirring often, until the sugar dissolves and the creamer is hot. Remove it from the heat add the liqueur and then the chocolate. Swirl the pot and then let the mixture sit for 30 seconds or so. Stir. If the chocolate is not melted, place the pot

If you're using any crumbly items, such as poundcake, it's best to pour a little fondue over them, rather than trying to skewer the pieces.

over the hot water. Continue to heat and stir, until all of the chocolate is melted.

2. Test the thickness of the fondue on a piece of fruit. If you prefer a thinner mixture, heat the remaining creamer in the microwave until it is about the same temperature as the fondue. Stir it into the chocolate and then transfer the mixture to the fondue pot. Keep the fondue warm over the lowest heat so that the chocolate doesn't burn. You can prepare and refrigerate the chocolate mixture up to two weeks in advance.

To reheat the fondue, microwave it on medium-low for a minute or two, until it's scoopable and then transfer it to the top of a double boiler. Heat over hot water until very warm. Transfer it to the fondue pot and continue as directed.

CHEEZECAKES

I like a cheezecake that is smooth and creamy throughout, with no grainy edges. The best way to accomplish this is to bake the cake in a waterbath (a Bain Marie). The results will be clearly worth the extra effort. This quintessential cheesecake has a mild tang from the sour cream substitute and just a hint of orange from the concentrate. I've paired it with a classic graham cracker crust, but you can use any nondairy crumb crust.

Sour Creem and Fruit Cheezecake

SERVES 12 – 16
MUST BE MADE 1 DAY AHEAD

Graham Cracker Crust

9 whole non-dairy graham crackers

5 tablespoons unsalted non-dairy stick margarine (such as Fleischmann's®), melted

Filling

3 eight-ounce packages Tofutti® Better Than Cream Cheese, softened 15 minutes at room temperature

1-1/8 cups sugar

1/2 cup Tofutti® Better Than Sour Cream

1-1/2 teaspoons orange juice concentrate, thawed

1 teaspoon vanilla extract

4 large eggs, room temperature

2 large egg yolks, room temperature

Strawberry Topping

1 pound strawberries, washed and hulled

1/2 teaspoon unflavored gelatin (*for kosher gelatin, directions follow)

2 teaspoons water

1/2 cup strained strawberry jam or jelly

Tips

To make cheezecake in a processor, place the cream cheese substitute in the processor bowl. Process until creamy. Add the sugar, and process until well mixed. Scrape down the bowl. Add the sour cream substitute, orange juice and vanilla. Pulse until blended. Add the eggs and egg yolks, and pulse until the eggs are incorporated. Scrape down the bowl, and then pulse until blended. Continue with step #4.

1. Preheat the oven to 350 degrees F. with a rack in the lower third of the oven. Grease a 9-inch springform pan. Have ready a pan big enough to hold the springform. Boil water to be used for a water-bath.

2. Crush the cookies in a plastic bag using a rolling pin (or in a food processor). Measure out 1-1/3 cups crumbs (packed) and discard any remainder. Stir the margarine into the crumbs, using just enough margarine for the crumbs to hold together when you press them together with your fingers (the exact amount will depend on the cookies used). Press the crumbs into the bottom of the springform pan. **Bake for 10 - 12 minutes** until the crust is just starting to brown. Cool until the pan can be handled. Wrap the outside of the pan with heavy-duty foil, bringing the edges up over the rim of the pan to secure it.

3. For the filling, place the cream cheese substitute in a mixer bowl and mix on low to medium speed until creamy. Beat in the sugar. Scrape down the bowl and beat a few seconds until well blended. Beat in the sour cream substitute, orange juice and vanilla. On low, beat in the eggs and yolks, two at a time, beating between additions, just until the eggs are incorporated.

4. Pour the batter into the crust. Place into the larger pan. Pour boiling water into the larger pan so that it comes halfway up

Tips

If using other fruits, choose a complimentary jam or jelly for the glaze. Currant or strawberry jelly works well with red fruits. Apricot or peach jam can be used for stone fruits or green fruits. Apple jelly is a neutral jelly that can work with anything.

Serve the cheezecake within several hours of arranging the fruit or the fruit may begin to weep. Do not freeze cheezecake.

*For a kosher glaze, use Diet Kojel® unflavored gelée. Place the berries on the cake first. Heat the strawberry jam with 2 teaspoons water until just starting to simmer. Stir in the gelée, and then brush the glaze on the fruit immediately.

the sides of the springform. **Bake for 80 - 90 minutes** until the cheezecake is set, but still quivers slightly. A toothpick inserted into the center will come out just barely clean. Remove the cheezecake from the water bath. Cool for about an hour and then refrigerate until completely cool. Cover with plastic wrap and chill overnight.

5. The next day, run a knife around the perimeter of the cheezecake and remove the springform ring. Gently place a paper towel on top of the cheezecake to mop up any liquid that has accumulated. Slice the strawberries, tip to stem, into 1/4-inch slices. Mix the gelatin and water together in a small bowl. Let it stand a few minutes to absorb the water and then microwave until liquidy and hot, about 15 seconds. Place the strawberry jam in a small pot and bring to a simmer over medium heat. Spoon in the gelatin mixture. Cook, while stirring, until the mixture is smooth and clear.

6. Arrange the strawberry slices on the top of the cake in concentric, overlapping circles. Brush the berries with the glaze, allowing it to pool on any exposed cheezecake. Refrigerate until the glaze sets, about 2 hours.

All of my testers were amazed when I told them that the cheezecake they were eating was dairy-free. It just seemed impossible that this rich cheezecake, topped with a spoonful of gooey pecan toffee topping, could be completely safe for someone allergic or lactose intolerant. But safe it is! The sauce is also superb on ice creem.

Pecan Toffee Cheezecake

SERVES 12 - 16
MUST BE MADE 1 DAY AHEAD

Shortbread Cookie Crumb Crust
12 non-dairy pecan shortbread cookies, such as Keebler® Sandies®
3-5 tablespoons unsalted non-dairy stick margarine (such as Fleischmann's®), melted

Filling
32 ounces Tofutti® Better than Cream Cheese, softened for 15 minutes at room temperature
1 cup granulated sugar
4 large eggs, room temperature
1 teaspoon vanilla extract

Pecan Toffee Topping
1-1/3 cups packed light brown sugar
4 tablespoons unsalted non-dairy stick margarine (such as Fleischmann's®), room temperature
2/3 cup Silk® soy creamer or non-dairy creamer, room temperature
1 tablespoon corn syrup
3/4 teaspoon vanilla extract
2/3 cup pecan pieces, toasted for 2 - 3 minutes until fragrant

Garnish (optional)
16 whole pecan halves

To make cheezecake in a processor, place the cream cheese substitute in the processor bowl. Process until creamy. Add the granulated sugar, and process until well mixed. Scrape down the bowl. Add the eggs and vanilla and pulse until blended. Scrape down the bowl, and then pulse until blended. Continue with step #4.

1. Heat the oven to 350 degrees F. with a rack in the lower third of the oven. Have a 9-inch springform pan ready. Have ready a pan big enough to hold the springform (such as a 12-inch square or round pan). Boil water to be used for a water-bath.

2. Crush the cookies in a plastic bag using a rolling pin (or use a food processor). Measure out 1-1/3 cups crumbs (packed), and discard any remainder. Stir the margarine into the crumbs, using just enough margarine for the crumbs to hold together when you press them together with your fingers (the exact amount will depend on the cookies used). Press the crumbs into the bottom of the springform pan. **Bake for 10 - 12 minutes** until the crust is just starting to brown. Cool until the pan can be handled and then wrap the outside of the pan with heavy-duty foil, bringing the edges up over the rim of the pan to secure it.

3. For the filling, place the Tofutti® in a mixer bowl and beat on low until blended. Beat in the granulated sugar. Scrape down the bowl and beat a few seconds. Add the eggs, two at a time, beating on low, just until the eggs are incorporated. Beat in the vanilla. (For processor directions, see sidebar).

4. Pour the batter into the crust. Place in the larger pan. Pour boiling water into the larger pan so that it comes halfway up the sides of the springform. **Bake for 75 - 85 minutes** until the cheezecake is set, but still quivers in the center. A toothpick

Unlike traditional caramel, this sauce gets stirred as it is simmering, which prevents the margarine from separating out upon refrigeration.

The cheezecake will keep in the refrigerator for several days. Do not freeze.

inserted into the center will come out just barely clean. Remove the cheezecake from the water bath. Cool for about an hour and then refrigerate until completely cool. Cover with plastic wrap and chill overnight.

5. For the sauce, combine the brown sugar, margarine, creamer and corn syrup in a small saucepan. Cook over medium heat, stirring occasionally until the mixture starts to simmer. Stirring continuously, simmer the sauce for 3 minutes. Remove the pot from the heat and stir in the vanilla. Let the sauce cool until just warm. Transfer to a storage container, cover and refrigerate overnight. Serve the sauce at room temperature or warmed, stirring in the toasted pecans just before serving.

6. To serve, run a knife around the perimeter of the cheesecake and remove the springform rim. Gently place a paper towel on top of the cheezecake to mop up any liquid that has accumulated. Let the cheezecake stand at room temperature for 15 - 20 minutes. To make the cheezecake more festive, lightly brush the pecan halves with a little of the sauce and then arrange them around the perimeter of the cheezecake. Serve each slice with a spoonful of topping, and pass the extra sauce.

Chocolate Lover's Cheezecake

SERVES 14 - 18

This very dense chocolate cheezecake is rich and smooth. The whipped topping not only makes it look delicious, it also tempers the intense chocolate flavor. For awesome variations, try Chocolate Pecan Toffee Cheezecake or German Chocolate Cheezecake.

Tea Biscuit Crumb Crust
3 tablespoons sugar
4 ounces non-dairy tea biscuits
7 tablespoons unsalted non-dairy stick margarine (such as Fleischmann's®), melted

Filling
3/4 cup dairy-case soymilk (such as Silk®)
1-1/2 cups sugar, divided
8 ounces non-dairy semisweet chocolate (see page 15, for brands), finely chopped
1/2 cup unsweetened Dutch processed cocoa powder
24 ounces Tofutti® Better Than Cream Cheese, room temperature
1 teaspoon vanilla
3 large eggs, room temperature
3 large egg yolks, room temperature

Garnish (optional)
1 carton Richwhip®, thawed
1 tablespoon of chocolate shavings

1. Heat the oven to 350 degrees F. with a rack in the lower third of the oven. Have a 9-inch springform pan ready. Have ready

Dutch-processed, or alkalized, co-coa powder is less acidic than regular cocoa. Here it creates a sweeter and more mellow filling. However, if you are unable to find it, use regular cocoa instead. Do not use sweet-ened cocoa or hot cocoa mix.

a pan big enough to hold the 9-inch springform (such as a 12-inch square or round pan). Boil water to be used for a water bath.

2. Place the sugar in a processor bowl and process for 30 - 60 seconds to finely grind the sugar. Transfer the sugar to a bowl. Place the cookies in the processor and pro-cess until they're finely ground. Measure out 1-1/2 cups crumbs. Stir in the sugar. Stir the margarine into the crumbs, add-ing just enough so that the crumbs hold together when you press them with your fingers (the exact amount will depend on the cookies used). Press the crumbs into the bottom of the springform pan. **Bake for 10 - 12 minutes** until the crust is just starting to brown. Cool until the pan can be handled and then wrap the outside of the pan with heavy-duty foil, bringing the edges up over the rim of the pan to secure it.

3. While the crust is baking, place the soy-milk and 3/4 cup sugar in a small pot. Heat over medium heat, stirring occa-sionally, until the sugar dissolves and the mixture just barely starts to simmer. Re-move it from the heat. Add the chopped chocolate. Let it stand for a minute and then stir until the chocolate melts. Stir in the cocoa. Strain the mixture into a bowl and set it aside to cool.

Tips

Before decorating, gently place a paper towel on top of the cheeze-cake to mop up any liquid that has accumulated. Run a knife around the perimeter of the cheezecake and then remove the springform ring. Whip the Richwhip® to stiff peaks and pipe the topping decoratively onto the cheezecake. If desired, dust the top with chocolate shavings.

This cheezecake is very rich, so you might want to serve small pieces.

Chocolate Cheezecake will keep in the refrigerator for several days. Do not freeze.

4. Place the Tofutti® in a mixer bowl and beat on low to medium speed until creamy. Beat in the remaining sugar until well mixed. Scrape down the bowl. Beat a few seconds to blend. On low, beat in the vanilla and the cooled chocolate mixture. Scrape down the bowl and beat a few more seconds.

5. Fork-whisk the eggs and yolks together in a small bowl. Add them to the cheezecake batter in 3 additions, beating on low to medium, just until the eggs are incorporated. Scrape down the bowl periodically. Pour the mixture over the crust. Place in the larger pan. Pour boiling water into the larger pan so that it comes halfway up the sides of the springform. **Bake for 80 - 90** minutes until a toothpick inserted into the center of the cheezecake tests clean, but the center of the cheezecake will look shiny and uncooked, and the center will be jiggly. Remove the cheezecake from the water bath, remove the foil and let the cheezecake sit at room temperature, until cool enough to refrigerate. Cover with plastic wrap and chill overnight.

VARIATIONS

Chocolate Pecan Toffee Cheezecake – use Pecan Toffee Topping (page 63)

German Chocolate Cheezecake – use 1/2 recipe of Coconut Pecan Filling (page 128)

This lovely cheezecake is lightly scented with rum and a hint of coconut. The sweet-tart pineapple topping provides nice texture and just the right amount of acidity. It's made in a large food processor, but can also be made in a mixer following the instructions in the previous recipe.

Piña Colada Cheezecake

SERVES 12 - 16
MAKE 1 DAY AHEAD

Graham Cracker Crust

9 whole non-dairy graham crackers

5 tablespoons unsalted non-dairy stick margarine (such as Fleischmann's®), melted

Filling

4 eight-ounce containers Tofutti® Better than Cream Cheese, softened at room temperature for 20 minutes

2/3 cup granulated sugar

1/4 cup coconut milk or Coco Lopez® Cream of Coconut (not a dairy product)

1 teaspoon vanilla extract

1 tablespoon dark rum

3 large eggs, room temperature

2 large egg yolks, room temperature

Pineapple Rum Topping

1 tablespoon cornstarch

1 tablespoon dark rum

2 eight-ounce cans crushed pineapple in juice

2 tablespoons packed brown sugar

1-2 tablespoons dark corn syrup, to taste

Tips

To make the cheezecake in the mixer, place the Tofutti in a mixer bowl and beat on low to medium speed until creamy. Scrape down the bowl. Beat a few seconds to blend. On low, beat in the sugar. Beat in the coconut milk, vanilla and rum. Scrape down the bowl. Fork-whisk together the eggs and egg yolks. Add them to the cheezecake batter in 3 additions, beating on low to medium until the eggs are incorporated. Continue with step #5

1. Preheat the oven to 350 degrees F. with a rack in the lower third of the oven. Have ready a 9-inch springform pan and another pan big enough to accommodate the springform. Boil water to be used for a water-bath.

2. Crush the cookies in a plastic bag using a rolling pin (or use a food processor). Measure out 1-1/3 cups crumbs, discarding any excess. Stir the margarine into the crumbs, using just enough margarine for the crumbs to hold together when you press them together with your fingers (the exact amount will depend on the cookies used). Press the crumbs into the bottom of the springform pan. **Bake for 10 - 12 minutes** until the crust is just starting to brown. Cool until the pan can be handled and then wrap the outside of the pan with heavy-duty foil, bringing the edges up over the rim of the pan to secure it.

3. For the filling, place the cream cheese substitute in the food processor bowl. Process until creamy. Add the granulated sugar and process until well mixed. Pour in the coconut milk or cream of coconut, vanilla and rum. Continue to process until well blended. Scrape the bowl down, and pulse a few times.

4. In a small bowl, whisk together the eggs and egg yolks. Pour into the processor. Pulse the mixture just until the eggs are incorporated. Scrape down the bowl and pulse again to blend everything.

Tips

To serve, run a knife around the perimeter of the cheesecake and remove the springform rim. Serve the cheezecake cold. Cheezecake may be stored, in the refrigerator, for up to 3 days. Do not freeze.

To cut cheezecake into nice slices, be sure to wipe off the blade between cuts.

5. Pour the batter into the prepared springform pan. Set the springform into the larger pan.

6. Pour boiling water into the larger pan to come 1/2 way up the sides of the springform. **Bake for 80 - 90 minutes** until the cheesecake is set, but still quivers in the center a little. A toothpick inserted into the center will come out just barely clean (if you underbake, the cheezecake will be quite creamy). Remove the cheezecake from the water-bath, remove the foil and let the cheezecake sit until cool enough to refrigerate. Cover and refrigerate overnight.

7. For the topping, place the cornstarch in a small pot. Stir in the rum and some of the pineapple juice to make a smooth mixture. Pour the remaining pineapple, juice, brown sugar and corn syrup into the pot. Bring to a boil over medium-high heat for 1 minute. Gently place a paper towel on top of the cheezecake to mop up any liquid that has accumulated. Pour the topping over the chilled cheezecake. Refrigerate the cheezecake overnight, or if the cheezecake has already been chilled overnight, then just until the topping is cold and firm (2 - 3 hours).

COOKIES AND BARS

These brownies are a snap to make and taste great when the chips are soft and melted, or later when they are firm. Because chocolate chips provide plenty of texture, the nuts can be omitted, if so desired. I use Reynolds® parchment paper to line the pan because it's kosher-certified to be non-dairy (no casein coating, as with some brands).

Chocolate Chip Brownies

MAKES 24 BARS

12 ounces non-dairy chocolate chips, divided (see page 15, for brands)
1/2 cup oil
1 cup sugar

3 large eggs, room temperature
1 teaspoon vanilla extract

1-1/4 cups all-purpose flour, fluffed, scooped and leveled into measuring cups
1/4 teaspoon baking soda
1/4 teaspoon salt

3/4 cup coarsely chopped walnuts or pecans

1. Preheat the oven to 350 degrees F. with a rack in the middle of the oven. Line the bottom of a 9 x 12-inch pan with kosher parchment paper (such as Reynolds®).

2. In a large micro wave-safe container, heat 1 cup chocolate chips and the oil on medium power for 2 minutes. Stir, and if the chocolate is not melted, heat for 1 minute more. Stir in the sugar. Set aside to cool.

3. Whisk the eggs and vanilla together in a small bowl. Whisk the egg mixture into the cooled chocolate mixture.

Tips

The brownies may be stored for several days, if wrapped in foil or plastic wrap. They will get drier as they sit, but are so moist when first baked, that they will still be wonderful even after several days.

To freeze for up to 3 months, wrap each brownie, individually, and then place in a plastic bag. Defrost the brownies, in their wrapping, at room temperature for several hours or overnight. If microwaving, remove the wrapping first.

4. In another small bowl, mix together the flour, baking soda and salt. Stir this into the chocolate mixture a little at a time. Stir in the remaining chocolate chips and nuts.

5. Spoon the batter into the prepared pan and **bake for 21 - 22 minutes** until a wooden skewer comes out with only a few moist crumbs attached.

6. Cool completely. Invert the pan onto a cutting board, re-invert so the brownies are right-side up and then cut the brownies into 2-inch bars.

These classic tasting brownies are made without leavening and mixed in an unorthodox way. They come out perfectly every time and do not have that too-soft center that is a problem with many brownies. They are excellent cold, and therefore make a great add-in to ice cream.

Fudgy Chewy Brownies

MAKES 24 BROWNIES

1 stick (8 tablespoons) unsalted non-dairy margarine (such as Fleischmann's®)
4 ounces non-dairy unsweetened chocolate (such as Hershey's®), finely chopped

4 large eggs, room temperature
2 cups sugar
1 teaspoon vanilla extract

1 cup all-purpose flour, fluffed, scooped and leveled into measuring cups
1/4 teaspoon salt
2-4 tablespoons unsweetened Dutch processed cocoa powder

1-1/2 cups coarsely chopped walnuts

1. Preheat the oven to 350 degrees F. with a rack in the middle of the oven. Line a 9 x 12-inch metal baking pan with aluminum foil, leaving 3 inches of overhang at each short end. Grease and flour the pan.

2. In a microwave-safe container, microwave the margarine until melted, about 1 minute. Add the chopped chocolate, and microwave for 1 minute on medium power. Stir, and microwave for 15-30 seconds more, until the chocolate is completely melted. Set aside to cool.

Tips

I prefer to cook brownies just a minute too long rather than a minute too short. If the edges are too dry after the first day they can always be cut off, but if undercooked, they're too soft for my taste.

For absolute perfection, eat these brownies within 2 days. To freeze for up to 3 months, wrap each brownie, individually and then place in a plastic bag. Defrost the brownies, in their wrapping, at room temperature for several hours or overnight. If microwaving, remove the wrapping first.

3. Place the eggs in a large mixer bowl. Using a balloon whisk attachment (if available), beat in the sugar, gradually, and continue to beat on medium-high until the mixture is fluffy and lightened in color and texture (about 5 minutes). Beat in the vanilla. Fold in the melted chocolate mixture.

4. Sift together the flour, salt and cocoa powder (within the range given, use the amount to suit your taste). Fold the flour mixture into the batter in 2 or 3 additions, until just incorporated. Gently stir in the nuts. Pour the batter into the prepared pan, spreading it gently to the corners. Shake the pan, lightly, to level the batter. **Bake for 26 - 30 minutes**, until a tester comes out almost completely clean and the top looks dull. Cool the cake, loosen the long edges and then lift the cake out of the pan using the foil. Cut the cake into 2 inch brownies.

This classic bar cookie is slightly chewy and studded with chocolate chips and nuts. If you can't find non-dairy chocolate chips, use non-dairy chocolate bars cut into small chunks.

Chocolate Chip Bars

SERVES 24

1-1/2 sticks (12 tablespoons) unsalted non-dairy margarine (such as Fleischmann's®), cold

1/2 cup granulated sugar

3/4 cup packed light brown sugar

1 large egg, room temperature

1 large egg yolk, room temperature

1 teaspoon vanilla extract

2 cups all-purpose flour, fluffed scooped and leveled

1/2 teaspoon salt

3/4 teaspoon baking soda

1- 1/2 cups non-dairy chocolate chips (see page 15, for brands)

1- 1/2 cups chopped walnuts or pecans

1. Preheat the oven to 350 degrees F. with a rack in the middle of the oven. Grease a 9 x 13-inch baking pan. Line the pan with kosher parchment paper (such as Reyn-olds®). Grease and flour the pan sides and the parchment paper. Set aside.

2. In a large mixer bowl, beat the margarine until creamy. Beat in the granulated and brown sugars, until the mixture is light

Tips

and fluffy (about 5 - 7 minutes). Beat in the egg and egg yolk, one at a time, until blended. Beat in the vanilla.

3. In a small bowl, mix together the flour, salt and baking soda. Dump the flour mixture into the batter. Beat on low, or stir the mixture by hand, just until the dry ingredients are almost incorporated. Add the chocolate chips and the nuts and continue to stir, or beat on low, until well mixed. Do not overbeat or the bars will be tough and dry.

4. With wet hands, pat the dough into the prepared pan. **Bake for 20 - 25 minutes** until the top is lightly browned and just past the shiny stage. A tester inserted into the center should come out with no crumbs attached. Cool the cake in the pan.

5. Loosen the edges with a knife or spatula. Invert onto a cutting board, cover with another cutting board and flip it over so that the cake is right-side-up. Cut into 2-inch squares.

This yummy bar has a shortbread cookie undercrust, a sweet-tart filling and a sweet and nutty crumb topping. A generous amount of raspberry filling is used so it doesn't get lost in the sandwich.

Raspberry Streusel Bars

SERVES 24

2 cups all-purpose flour, fluffed, scooped
   and leveled into measuring cups
3/4 cup granulated sugar
1/8 teaspoon salt
2 sticks (16 tablespoons) unsalted non-dairy
   margarine (such as Fleischmann's®), frozen
   and cut into 1/4-inch pieces

Topping

1 cup all-purpose flour, fluffed, scooped and
   leveled into a measuring cup
1/2 cup packed light brown sugar
3/4 cup coarsely chopped pecans
10 tablespoons unsalted non-dairy stick
   margarine, melted

Filling
1-1/2 cups seedless raspberry jam

1. Preheat the oven to 375 degrees F. with a rack in the upper third of the oven. Line a 9 x 13-inch baking pan with aluminum foil, leaving a 3-inch overhang at each short end. Grease the foil.

2. Place 2 cups flour, granulated sugar and salt in a food processor bowl. Pulse to combine the ingredients. Add the marga-

These bars will keep for a day or two at room temperature, if well wrapped in plastic wrap. The topping will soften a bit if the air is humid Do not freeze.

rine, and pulse on and off, until the mixture looks like coarse crumbs. Press the dough into the pan and refrigerate for 15 minutes.

3. Combine all of the topping ingredients. Stir with a fork until moistened and then pinch the dough to form clumps. Set aside.

4. **Bake the crust for 15-20 minutes,** until just starting to brown. Spread the jam over the hot crust. Sprinkle the topping over the jam. **Bake 15 – 25 minutes** until browned and bubbly. Cool on a wire rack. Use the foil to lift the pastry out of the pan, set it on a cutting board and cut into 2-inch squares.

It took over 200 cookies until I got this recipe exactly the way I wanted it. Because they bake for only 5 or 6 minutes the sugar wasn't dissolving properly and the cookies tasted gritty. The solution, was to melt the margarine first, and to use powdered sugar, instead of granulated sugar. Chilling the dough also helps, as the chilled dough gets to cook longer. The cookies bake down into perfectly round, smooth and fudgy discs. They're lovely to look at and a delight to eat. Thanks go to Fiama and Fabio Pschaidt, the children who helped me taste-test the cookies.

Chocolate Chocolate Chip Cookies

MAKES 75 COOKIES

24 ounces (4 cups) non-dairy chocolate chips, divided (if using bar chocolate, finely chop half, and cut half into small chunks)
2 sticks (16 tablespoons) non-dairy unsalted margarine (such as Fleischmann's®), room temperature
1 cup packed light brown sugar
1/2 cup powdered sugar
1 teaspoon vanilla extract
3 large eggs, room temperature

2-3/4 cups all-purpose flour, fluffed, scooped and leveled into measuring cups
1 teaspoon baking soda
1/4 teaspoon salt

1 cup coarsely chopped nuts, optional

1. Preheat the oven to 375 degrees F. with racks in the upper and lower thirds of the oven. Line 2 cookie sheets with kosher parchment paper (such as Reynolds®). Cut 2 more sheets of parchment to the same size and set them aside.

If you are allergic, use kosher parchment paper because other parchment might be coated with casein, a dairy product that is okay for lactose intolerancy, but not for allergy.

The cookies may be stored at room temperature, in a covered container, for up to 3 days. Freeze them, individually wrapped, for up to 3 months. Defrost wrapped cookies at room temperature, or unwrap and microwave-defrost for 10 seconds, or until thawed.

2. Place the margarine in a large microwave-safe bowl. Microwave on high for 1 minute, until the margarine is melted. Stir in 2 cups (12 ounces) chocolate chips. Microwave on medium for 1 minute, stir and then reheat if the chocolate is not melted. Stir in the sugars and the vanilla. Let the chocolate mixture stand until it is just tepid, about 5 minutes. Whisk in the eggs, one at a time.

3. In a small bowl, sift together the flour, baking soda and salt. Add the flour mixture, all at once, to the chocolate mixture. Stir until the dry ingredients are just incorporated. Stir in the remaining chocolate chips and the nuts. Chill the dough for 10 – 20 minutes until it is just firm enough to form into balls.

4. Pinch off enough dough to form a 1-inch ball (about the size of a malted milk ball). Roll the dough lightly between the palms of your hands until it is round and smooth, and then flatten it, between your palms, to about 1/2-inch thick. Place the balls on the parchment, leaving 1 inch between cookies. Place two cookie sheets in the oven, and bake for 3 minutes. Move the top cookie sheet to the lower rack and the lower cookie sheet to the top. Bake for 2-3 minutes more until the cookies are just barely done and the tops just lose their shine. Slide the parchment onto cooling racks. Repeat with the remaining dough.

Linzer Tarts

MAKES 35 COOKIES

Unlike pale, bakery-made linzer tart giants, these dainty cookies are lightly scented with cinnamon and clove. The hint of spice nicely compliments the almond dough and raspberry filling.

3 sticks (24 tablespoons) unsalted non-dairy margarine (such as Fleischmann's®), softened until pliable (about 15 minutes)
1 cup sugar
2 teaspoons vanilla extract

2 cups slivered almond
3 cups all-purpose flour, fluffed, scooped and leveled into measuring cups
1/2 teaspoon cinnamon
1/2 teaspoon cloves

1 jar seedless raspberry jam
Powdered sugar for sprinkling

1. In a medium mixer bowl, beat the margarine until creamy. Add the sugar and beat 3 - 5 minutes, until lightened in color and very fluffy. Beat in the vanilla.

2. In a food processor, pulse the almonds and flour until the almonds are finely ground. Add the cinnamon and cloves. Pulse to blend. Beat the flour mixture into the margarine mixture just until blended. Wrap the dough in plastic wrap and refrigerate it overnight.

3. Preheat the oven to 325 degrees F. with a rack in the middle of the oven. Line insulated cookie sheets with kosher parchment paper (such as Reynolds®).

Linzer tarts keep for several days at room temperature, in a covered container. They may be frozen in one layer, on a cookie sheet, and then transfered to a storage container or plastic bag. This way they won't freeze together and you'll be able to defrost them one at a time. They'll keep frozen for 3 months. Defrost them at room temperature, uncovered.

4. You can roll the dough in any traditional manner with which you are familiar, or use this fail-proof technique: Cut open a jumbo zip-top bag so that it is hinged on one long side. Flour the inside of the plastic and add 1/4 of the dough. Roll to 1/8-inch thickness, flipping the plastic over and flouring the dough as necessary. Using a 1-1/2-inch round cookie cutter, cut the dough into rounds. Cut out the centers of half of the cookies using the back of a pastry tip or a 1/2-inch cookie cutter. Place on the cookie sheet and **bake for 15 minutes** until lightly browned. Slide the parchment onto cooling racks and let the cookies cool. While one sheet of cookies is baking, roll out and cut another piece of dough.

5. Dust the top cookies (with the holes) with powdered sugar. Spread the other cookies with jam and sandwich the two together.

Pecan Snowballs

MAKES 48 COOKIES

2 cups all-purpose flour, fluffed, scooped
   and leveled into measuring cups
2-1/3 cups (9 ounces) pecan pieces

2 sticks (16 tablespoons) unsalted non-
   dairy margarine (such as Fleischmann's®),
   softened until pliable (about 15 minutes)
1/2 cup sugar
1-1/2 teaspoons vanilla extract

1-2 cups powdered sugar

1. Preheat the oven to 350 degrees F. with oven racks in the upper and lower thirds of the oven. Line 2 cookie sheets with kosher parchment paper (such as Reynolds®). Cut two more pieces of parchment to fit the cookie sheets and set them aside.

2. In a food processor pulse the flour and the pecans until the nuts are finely ground.

3. In a large mixer bowl beat the margarine until creamy (about 2 - 3 minutes). Add the sugar and beat for 2 minutes on medium speed. Beat in the vanilla. On low, beat in the flour mixture, all at once, and beat until the dough comes together. Scrape down the sides of the bowl and beat for a few seconds more.

These are my all-time favorite cookies. Many recipes like this have no sugar in the dough itself, but I prefer to include it, so that you have sweetness within and without. It also makes for a more "toothy" cookie. I bake the cookies a bit longer than is traditional because browned dough delivers more of a flavor punch.

The snowballs may be stored in a plastic container or plastic bag for several days. They may be frozen in one layer, on a cookie sheet, and then transfered to a storage container or plastic bag. This way they won't freeze together and you'll be able to defrost them one at a time. They'll keep frozen for 3 months. Frozen balls are great right from the freezer or can be defrosted at room temperature, or in the microwave (on defrost).

4. Pinch off enough dough to form a 1-inch ball (about the size of a malted milk ball). Roll the dough lightly between the palms of your hands until it is round and smooth. Place on the prepared cookie sheet. Repeat with the remaining dough, spacing the balls 1 – 2 inches apart on both cookie sheets and the extra parchment.

5. **Bake for 10 minutes.** Move the top cookie sheet down to the bottom rack and the bottom sheet up. **Bake 10 - 15** minutes more until the balls are just starting to brown and are firm to the touch. Slide the parchment onto cooling racks and let the cookies cool for 5 - 10 minutes. Meanwhile, slide the parchment with the remaining dough onto the cookie sheets, and bake and finish as with the other cookies.

6. Place the powdered sugar in a shallow bowl (the amount you will need depends on the depth of the bowl). Place a couple of the cookies in the sugar and roll them around until well coated. Repeat with remaining balls. Discard excess powdered sugar as it will have bits of pecans and fat in it that can spoil. Cool the cookies completely before eating or storing.

Rugelach

This Jewish cookie is a cream cheese, flaky pastry, filled with cinnamon, sugar, nuts and preserves. Homemade ones are usually crescent shaped, but it's easier to shape them into logs. My trick to making moist cookies is to use the chunks of apricot that most recipes say to strain out.

Dough

2-1/4 cups all-purpose flour, fluffed, scooped and leveled into measuring cups

1/4 cup powdered sugar

Pinch salt

2 sticks (16 tablespoons) unsalted non-dairy margarine (such as Fleischmann's®), frozen

1/2 pound Tofutti® Better than Cream Cheese, cold

1/2 teaspoon vanilla

Filling

1-1/2 cups pecan pieces

3/4 cup sugar

1-1/2 teaspoons cinnamon

8 ounces apricot preserves, room temperature

3/4 cup raisins

1/4 cup unsalted non-dairy stick margarine

2 teaspoons vegetable oil

1. For the dough, place the flour, powdered sugar and salt in a food processor bowl and pulse to mix the ingredients together. Cut the margarine into 1/4-inch chunks, add to the processor and pulse on and off, until the mixture looks like coarse meal. Cut the cream cheese substitute into 1/4-inch chunks and add to the proces-

Tips

Unlike butter, margarine does not melt out into a clear, oily liquid. Therefore, when you need to use margarine for brushing or glazing, combine it with a little oil to make it more liquidy.

Some of the apricot jam leaks out of these cookies and can burn before the cookies are done baking. For this reason, I recommend using insulated cookie sheets. If you do not have any, try nesting two cookie sheets together to try and simulate the effect of having an insulated sheet.

sor. (If it's too soft to cut, add it by table-spoonful to the processor.) Add the vanilla. Pulse until the dough just starts to come together. Turn the dough out onto a board and press it together. Shape the dough into a disc, wrap in plastic wrap and refrigerate overnight.

2. Preheat the oven to 375 degrees F. with a rack in the middle of the oven. Line insulated cookie sheets with kosher parchment paper (such as Reynolds®).

3. For the filling, combine the pecans, sugar and cinnamon in a processor bowl. Pulse on and off, until the nuts are coarsely chopped. Remove 2/3 of the filling and set it aside. Pulse the remaining mixture until the nuts are finely ground. This will be the topping.

4. Place the margarine and oil in a microwave-safe bowl with a cover. Microwave on high for 30 seconds, or until the margarine is melted.

5. For logs: Roll 1/4 of the dough (7 ounces) into a rectangle 1/16-inch thick x 5-inches wide x 10-inches long. Brush it with apricot preserves to within 1/4-inch of the top edge. Cut any large chunks of apricot into smaller pieces and distribute them evenly over the dough. Sprinkle 2 - 3 heaping tablespoons of pecan filling (coarsely chopped mixture) over the preserves. Place some raisins in a line on the

For a foolproof method of rolling out dough, cut open a jumbo zip-top bag so that it is hinged on one long side. Flour the inside. Roll the dough inside of the bag, flipping it over, flouring the dough and releasing the plastic as necessary.

One nice way to cut the logs into even pieces is to get an artist's cutting mat that is marked off in a 1-inch grid. You can also get a clear plastic cutting board and mark off the increments on one side.

long edge of the dough. Sprinkle another tablespoon of raisins evenly over the dough. Roll the dough up from the edge with the raisins towards the clean edge. Press lightly on the roll so that the bottom edge will seal well. If it fails to seal, brush it with some of the melted margarine and then press on the dough to seal it. Place the roll on waxed paper. Brush it with some of the melted margarine mixture and sprinkle liberally with the topping so that the whole roll, except the bottom, is coated. Cut the log into pieces slightly larger than 1 inch.

6. For crescents: Cut the dough in half. Roll the dough into a 12-inch circle, about 1/16-inch thick (see sidebar for rolling technique). Spread half of the preserves over the dough, cutting up any large chunks. Sprinkle on half of the filling. Cut the dough into 16 equal wedges, wiping off the blade with a damp cloth between cuts. Place 2 or 3 raisins at the base of each triangle and then scatter the remaining raisins over the dough. Roll the cookies up, from the wide end of each triangle to the tip. Bend the cookies, slightly, to create crescents. Transfer the crescents to waxed paper. Brush with some of the melted margarine mixture and sprinkle liberally with the topping.

7. Place the cookies on the prepared cookie sheets. Logs should be placed, seam size

The cookies may be stored in a covered container for several days. They may be frozen in one layer, on a cookie sheet, and then transfered to a storage container or plastic bag. This way they won't freeze together and you'll be able to defrost them one at a time. They'll keep frozen for 3 months. Defrost at room temperature, in a covered container, for several hours or overnight.

down (with the spiral perpendicular to the cookie sheet - see drawing, below).

8. **Bake 25 - 30 minutes** or until nicely browned. Slide the parchment paper onto a cooling rack and allow the cookies to cool. If the preserves that have oozed out are very dark or burned, remove the cookies from the parchment paper before they cool, as this sticky stuff will cling to each cookie and may not taste good if it is burned. While one sheet of cookies is baking, prepare another batch of cookies.

Mandel Bread

MAKES 24 - 35 COOKIES

Although "mandel" means almond in Yiddish, these Jewish cookies are often made with other nuts. Twice baked, they are similar to biscotti, and are wonderful accompanied by a nice cup of tea or coffee.

2 cups all-purpose flour, fluffed, scooped
  and leveled into measuring cups
1/4 cup slivered almonds
1 teaspoon baking powder

2 large eggs, room temperature
1/2 cup canola or nut oil
1/2 teaspoon vanilla extract
1/4 teaspoon pure almond extract (optional)
1/2 cup sugar

1/3 cup raisins
1/2 cup coarsely chopped almonds or
  pecans, toasted for 2 – 3 minutes until
  fragrant

1 tablespoon sugar, mixed with 1/4 teaspoon
  cinnamon

1. Preheat the oven to 350 degrees F. with a rack in the middle of the oven. Grease two cookie sheets.

2. Process the flour, almonds and baking powder until the almonds are finely ground.

3. In a large mixer bowl, beat together the eggs, oil, vanilla and almond extract. Beat in 1/2 cup sugar until blended.

4. Dump the flour mixture into the egg mixture and mix (or beat on low) together

Mandel Bread will harden as they cool. Store them in an airtight container for up to 2 weeks. They may be frozen in one layer, on a cookie sheet, and then transfered to a storage container or plastic bag. This way they won't freeze together and you'll be able to defrost them one at a time. They'll keep frozen for 3 months. Defrost the cookies at room temperature, uncovered.

until almost thoroughly blended. In a small bowl, soak the raisins in hot water for 1 minute. Drain, squeeze dry and add the raisins to the dough along with the chopped almonds or pecans. Mix or beat on low just until well blended.

5. Divide the dough in half. On a floured board, shape each half into a loaf, 1-1/2-inches wide, 3/4-inch thick and about 10-inches long. Transfer the loaves to one of the prepared cookie sheets. **Bake for 30 minutes.** Cool for 5 minutes.

6. Transfer the loaves to a cutting board. Using a serrated knife, slice the dough, on the diagonal, into 3/8-inch thick pieces. Depending on the degree of slant, the slices will be between 2-1/2 to 4-inches long (your preference).

7. Place the cookies flat on the prepared cookie sheets. Sprinkle each slice with some cinnamon-sugar. **Bake for 7 minutes**. Turn the cookies over, sprinkle with cinnamon-sugar, and **bake for another 5 - 7 minutes** until the cookies are lightly browned. Let the cookies cool right on the hot cookie sheets.

Hazelnut Almond Biscotti

MAKES 24 – 35 COOKIES

1/2 cup slivered almonds

1/2 cup unsalted non-dairy margarine, softened until pliable (about 15 minutes)
3/4 cup sugar
2 large eggs, room temperature
1/2 teaspoon vanilla extract
1/4 teaspoon pure almond extract (optional)

2-1/4 cups all-purpose flour, fluffed, scooped and leveled into measuring cups
1 teaspoon baking powder

1/2 cup skinned hazelnuts, coarsely chopped

1. Preheat the oven to 350 degrees F. with a rack in the middle of the oven. Grease two cookie sheets.

2. Bake the almonds for 3 - 5 minutes until fragrant and just starting to brown. Cool them and chop coarsely. Set aside.

3. Place the margarine and sugar in a mixer bowl and beat until lightened in color and texture, about 3 minutes. Beat in the eggs, one at a time, until incorporated. Beat in the vanilla and the almond extract.

Biscotti will harden as they cool. They may be stored in an airtight container for up to 2 weeks. They may be frozen in one layer, on a cookie sheet, and then transfered to a storage container or plastic bag. This way they won't freeze together and you'll be able to defrost them one at a time. They'll keep frozen for 3 months. Defrost the cookies at room temperature, uncovered.

4. In another bowl, thoroughly mix together the flour and baking powder. Dump the flour mixture into the egg mixture and mix (or beat on low) until almost thoroughly blended. Stir in the hazelnuts and reserved almonds. Refrigerate the dough for about 1 hour. Scrape the dough out and divide in half. Using wet hands, squeeze each half into a loaf, 1-1/2-inches wide, 3/4-inch thick and about 10 inches long. Transfer the loaves to one of the greased cookie sheets. **Bake for 30 minutes**. Cool 5 minutes. Transfer the loaves to a cutting board. Using a serrated knife, slice the dough, on the diagonal, into 3/8-inch thick pieces. Depending on the degree of slant, the slices will be between 2-1/2 to 4 inches long (your preference). Place the cookies flat on the prepared cookie sheets. **Bake for 15 minutes** until the cookies are lightly browned. Let the cookies cool right on the hot cookie sheets.

VARIATIONS

Other nuts may be substituted for the hazelnuts and almonds, or add 1/4 cup raisins, dried cranberries, chocolate chips, or dried cherries. Vary the flavor by adding 1/2 teaspoon orange oil, vanilla, Kahlúa, or Grand Marnier (see page 28, for kosher liqueurs). In addition to any of the above, you can add spices to taste, such as: 1/2 teaspoon chopped fresh lavender, 1/4 teaspoon black pepper, 1/2 teaspoon ginger, 1/2 teaspoon cinnamon, etc.

Pecan Chocolate Sandwiches

MAKES 25 COOKIE SANDWICHES

1 cup pecans, toasted at 350 degrees F. until fragrant (about 3 minutes)
1/2 cup sugar

1-1/2 sticks (12 tablespoons) unsalted, non-dairy margarine (such as Fleischmann's®), softened until pliable (about 15 minutes)
1/2 teaspoon vanilla extract
1-1/2 cups all-purpose flour, fluffed, scooped and leveled into measuring cups

4 ounces non-dairy semisweet chocolate, (see page 15, for brands) finely chopped
1 teaspoon oil

1. Place the nuts and sugar in a food processor. Pulse until the nuts are finely ground. Add the margarine and vanilla, and pulse until well mixed. Add the flour, and pulse on and off, until the mixture starts to form a ball. Scrape the dough out of the processor onto a piece of plastic wrap. Wrap the dough tightly and chill overnight.

2. Preheat the oven to 350 degrees F. with racks in the lower and upper thirds of the oven. Line two cookie sheets with kosher parchment paper (such as Reynolds®).

These cookies taste a little like Milano® cookies, although these contain pecans which add a wonderful buttery flavor and great texture to the cookie.

You can sandwich the cookies with pure chocolate or mix in a little oil (as I have done). Adding the oil makes the chocolate spread a little easier, and makes it a tad softer and less brittle. Either method works fine.

The cookies may be stored for a few days in a sealed container or plastic bag. They may be frozen in one layer, on a cookie sheet, and then transfered to a storage container or plastic bag. This way they won't freeze together and you'll be able to defrost them one at a time. They'll keep frozen for 3 months. Defrost at room temperature, unwrapped.

Cut two more pieces of parchment to fit the cookie sheets, and set them aside.

3. For a foolproof rolling method, cut open a jumbo zip-top bag so that it is hinged on one long side. Flour the inside of the plastic and place 1/3 of the dough inside. Roll the dough to 1/16-inch thickness, flipping the plastic over and flouring the dough as necessary.

4. Cut out cookies using a 2-inch oval cookie cutter or a 1-1/4-inch round cutter. Place on the cookie sheets. Repeat with the remaining dough, placing them on both cookie sheets and on the extra parchment.

5. **Bake for 7 minutes.** Move the top cookie sheet to the lower rack and the bottom sheet to the top. **Bake for 6-8 minutes** more or until light brown. Slide the parchment paper onto cooling racks. Slide the parchment with the remaining dough onto the cookie sheets, and bake as with the first batch.

6. Put the chocolate and oil in a microwave-safe container. Microwave on medium power until the chocolate melts (about 1 - 2 minutes). Stir until the chocolate and oil are well combined.

7. Spread a thin layer of chocolate onto half of the cookies. Set a plain cookie on top of each chocolate one to make a sandwich.

From this one recipe, you get three different cookies: a ball cookie with a cherry, a slice-and-bake cookie with nuts, cinnamon and sugar topping or a rolled cookie-cutter cookie drizzled with chocolate, or glazed. To make all three kinds, you'll want to double the recipe.

Buttery Cookies with 3 Variations

MAKES 25 – 60 COOKIES
MAKE THE FREEZER AND ROLLED COOKIE DOUGH 1 DAY AHEAD

Dough

1/4 cup powdered sugar

1/4 cup granulated sugar

2-1/2 cups all-purpose flour, fluffed, scooped and leveled into measuring cups

2 sticks plus 3 tablespoons (19 tablespoons total) unsalted non-dairy margarine (such as Fleischmann's®), cold

1/2 teaspoon vanilla extract

Cherry Flowers

25 candied cherries

Freezer Slice-and-Bake Cookies

1/2 cup pecan pieces

1 tablespoon sugar

1/2 teaspoon cinnamon

1 large egg white, whisked with 1 teaspoon water (not for vegan)

For Rolled Cookie-Cutter Cookies

2 ounces non-dairy semisweet chocolate, (see page 15, for brands) finely chopped

1/2 teaspoon oil

Uncooked slice-and-bake logs can be frozen for 3 months. Place the wrapped logs in a plastic bag.

To roll dough to an even thickness, I use a plastic dough-ring that is exactly 1/8-inch thick. The rolling pin runs on the outer edges of the ring allowing the dough to be rolled to exactly that thickness. I also have a dough board with adjustable edges that creates different thicknesses for rolling. If you can't find either of these, you can make your own guides by using strips of wood the thickness you need.

1. For the dough, mix the powdered sugar, granulated sugar and flour in a large mixer bowl. Cut the cold margarine into 1/4-inch cubes. Add to the mixer bowl and mix on low speed until crumbly. Add the vanilla. Continue to mix on low speed until the dough just starts to come together. Turn it out onto a board.

2. For the Cherry Flowers, preheat the oven to 375 degrees F. with racks in the lower and upper thirds of the oven. Shape the dough into 1–inch balls. Place the balls on cookie sheets lined with kosher parchment paper (such as Reynolds®). Press a cherry into the center of each ball. The dough will flatten and crack at the edges. Bake for 7 minutes. Move the top cookie sheet to the lower rack, and the bottom sheet to the top. Bake for 8-10 minutes more until the cookies are firm and browned on the bottom (the tops will not brown). Slide the parchment paper onto cooling racks.

3. For the Freezer Cookies, divide the dough in half. Form each half into a 9 x 1-1/4-inch log. Wrap each log in waxed paper and freeze the logs at least overnight. When ready to bake, preheat the oven to 375 degrees F. Line 2 cookie sheets with parchment paper. Process the nuts, sugar and cinnamon until finely ground. Cut the logs into 1/8-inch slices. Place the slices on the cookie sheets. Brush the

Parchment paper is not essential for these cookies, but I always use it because the paper can be slid onto the cooling racks rather than having to transfer each cookie. Some parchment paper is coated with a casein product, so look for parchment paper that is non-dairy, kosher-certified (Reynolds®). If you are simply lactose intolerant, you can use any parchment paper.

cookies with the egg white mixture and sprinkle with the nut mixture. **Bake for 7 minutes.** Move the top cookie sheet to the lower rack, and the bottom sheet to the top. **Bake for 5-8 minutes** more until the cookies are browning on top. Alternatively, you can leave the slices plain and decorate them as described below.

4. For the Rolled Cookies, gather the dough into a flattened ball. Wrap it in plastic wrap and refrigerate overnight. Preheat the oven to 375 degrees F. Line two cookie sheets with kosher parchment paper (such as Reynolds®). Cut open a jumbo zip-top bag so that it is hinged on one long side. Flour the inside of the plastic and place the dough inside. Roll to a scant 1/8-inch thickness, flipping the plastic over and flouring the dough as necessary. Cut out cookies using cookie cutters of your choice. Place cookies on the parchment paper. **Bake for 7 minutes.** Move the top cookie sheet to the lower rack and the bottom sheet to the top. **Bake for 5-8 minutes** more until the cookies are browning on top. Slide the parchment onto cooling racks.

5. To decorate, place the chocolate and oil in a small, microwave-safe bowl. Microwave on medium for 1 minute. Stir. If the chocolate isn't melted, heat in 15 second increments, until melted. Scrape the chocolate into a small, disposable deco-

Tips

Vanilla Icing

Sift 2 cups powdered sugar into a mixer bowl. Beat in 1 teaspoon vanilla extract and 3 tablespoons plus 1 teaspoon Silk® soy creamer or non-dairy creamer. Divide the icing into bowls and add food coloring of choice.

rating bag or a parchment cone. Make a tiny snip in the end and then drizzle the chocolate over the cookies. Alternatively, you can use icing alone (see sidebar) or with sprinkles, or you can decorate with nuts, as in the freezer variation.

These simple buttery cookies can be made in about 10 minutes, and are ready to eat in about an hour. A pecan half hides the raspberry preserves within the cookie ball.

Raspberry Surprise Cookies

MAKES 35 COOKIES

2-1/2 sticks (20 tablespoons) unsalted non-dairy margarine (such as Fleischmann's®), cold

3/4 cup sugar

2 large egg yolks, room temperature

1 teaspoon vanilla extract

3 cups all-purpose flour, fluffed, spooned and leveled into measuring cups

4 tablespoons seedless raspberry preserves

35 pecan halves

1. Preheat the oven to 375 degrees F. with racks in the upper and lower thirds of the oven. Line two cookie sheets with kosher parchment paper (such as Reynolds®). Cut 2 more sheets of parchment to the same size and set them aside.

2. Place the margarine in a large mixer bowl. Beat on medium speed to soften and blend it slightly. Gradually beat in the sugar. Continue to beat the mixture on medium speed, until lightened in texture and color (about 3 - 5 minutes).

3. Beat in the egg yolks, one at a time, until well blended. Beat in the vanilla. Add the flour all at once, and beat on low until the dough starts to come together. Using

Butter is often used at room temperature, but because margarine is much softer than butter, it works better when you start it colder and let the beating process soften it up.

your hands, knead the dough until well mixed and smooth.

4. Pinch off enough dough to form a 1-inch ball (about the size of a malted milk ball). Roll the dough lightly between the palms of your hands until it's round and smooth. Place on the cookie sheets about 2 inches apart from each other. Using the end of a wooden spoon, make an indentation in the center of each cookie. Wiggle the handle back and forth to enlarge the hole to about 1/4-inch wide and deep. Fill the holes with raspberry preserves. Press a pecan half on top of each hole. **Bake for 7 minutes**. Move the top cookie sheet to the lower rack and the bottom sheet to the top. **Bake for 6-8 minutes** more until the cookies are firm but un-browned on top. Slide the parchment onto cooling racks.

Easy Cookie-Cutter Cookies

I originally developed this dough as a service project for the children of our Temple who were going to provide cookies for 1000 needy children. We wanted a dough that would set up quickly and be easy for the children to roll. This cookie was perfect. The dough chills for only 15 minutes and then rolls out without sticking. For the tops you can use a very simple icing or coat them with chocolate and nuts.

MAKES 50 - 80

3 sticks (24 tablespoons) unsalted non-dairy margarine (preferably Fleischmann's®), softened at room temperature for 15 - 20 minutes
1-1/2 cups sugar
1 teaspoon salt
1 teaspoon vanilla
1 large egg, room temperature

4 cups all-purpose flour, fluffed, scooped and leveled into measuring cups

Up to 4 teaspoons room temperature water, if needed

Vanilla Icing
2 cups powdered sugar
1 teaspoon vanilla extract
3 tablespoons plus 1 teaspoon Silk® soy creamer or non-dairy creamer
Food coloring, sprinkles, etc for decorating

1. Preheat the oven to 350 degrees F. with racks in the bottom and top thirds of the oven. Line 2 cookie sheets with kosher parchment paper (such as Reynolds®).

2. In a large mixer bowl beat together the

To get an even thickness of dough, I use a plastic dough ring that is exactly 1/8-inch thick. The rolling pin runs on the edges of the ring, allowing the dough to be rolled to exactly that thickness.

margarine, sugar, salt and vanilla extract on low to medium speed, just until well blended.

3. Break the egg into a small bowl and fork-whisk until blended. Gradually beat the egg into the margarine mixture.

4. Add the flour, all at once, to the mixer bowl, and beat on low speed until the mixture comes together into a dough. If the dough does not form, add the water a little at a time, using just enough to bring the dough together. Press the dough into a ball, wrap in plastic, and refrigerate for 15 minutes.

5. Cut the dough into 4 pieces and return 3 pieces to the refrigerator.

6. For a foolproof rolling method, cut open a jumbo zip-top bag so that it is hinged on one long side. Flour the inside of the plastic and place one piece of dough inside. Roll to 1/8-inch thick or slightly thinner, flipping the plastic over and flouring the dough as necessary.

7. Cut out the dough using cookie cutters of your choice. Set the cookies on the prepared cookie sheets. **Bake for 7 minutes**. Move the top cookie sheet to the lower rack and the bottom sheet to the top. **Bake for another 7 - 9 minutes**, until the cookies are nicely browned around the edges. Slide the parchment onto cooling racks. Repeat the process using the rest of the dough.

To make a harder icing for cookies that need to be stacked or frozen, use this icing:

Royal Icing

Mix together 3 large pasteurized egg whites, 3-3/4 cups sifted powdered sugar, 1/2 teaspoon cream of tartar and 1/2 teaspoon flavoring of choice. Beat for 7-10 minutes until the icing holds a strong peak. Add 1/4 cup more powdered sugar if necessary. Keep the frosting covered with a damp cloth to keep it from drying out. To use Royal Icing, outline the cookies and then let them dry. Thin some icing with water until it is the consistency of heavy cream. Using a teaspoon or squeeze bottle, fill in from the outline inward to cover the area. Let the cookies set for 1 hour before adding designs.

8. For the icing, sift the powdered sugar into a mixer bowl. Beat in the vanilla and creamer. Divide the icing into several small bowls and add food coloring of choice to each bowl. The icing thickens as it sits, so keep the bowl covered until ready to use. Add a little more creamer if the icing gets too thick. Spread the icing onto the cookies using a small spreader. Sprinkles and such should be sprinkled on while the frosting is still wet. To add raised designs, let the glaze set and then make a thicker icing that can be piped onto the glazed cookies.

This soft, slightly chewy peanut butter cookie is made with margarine instead of shortening to eliminate the waxy mouth-feel of a standard peanut butter cookie. Reduced sugar and extra beating time help create a thick, soft cookie.

Peanut Butter Crosshatch Cookies

MAKES 20 COOKIES

1 stick (8 tablespoons) non-dairy unsalted margarine (such as Fleischmann's®), softened until pliable (about 15 minutes)
3/4 cup peanut butter
1 cup packed light brown sugar
1 large egg, room temperature
1 teaspoon vanilla extract
1-1/2 cups all-purpose flour, fluffed, scooped and leveled into measuring cups.
3/4 teaspoon baking soda
1/4 teaspoon salt

1. Preheat the oven to 375 degrees F. with a rack in the middle of the oven. Line three baking sheets with kosher parchment paper (such as Reynolds®).

2. In a large mixer bowl, on low speed, beat together the margarine and peanut butter. Beat in the brown sugar, on medium speed, until the mixture is well mixed and fluffy (about 3 minutes). Mix the egg and vanilla together in a small bowl. Gradually beat the egg mixture into the margarine mixture until well blended.

3. In a small bowl, stir together the flour, baking soda and salt. Add to the batter all at once. Beat on low, or stir in by hand,

These cookies are meltingly tender. They're perfect when freshly baked, but can be stored in a covered container for 2 days. Freeze them, individually wrapped, for up to 3 months. Defrost wrapped cookies at room temperature, or unwrap and microwave-defrost for 10 seconds, or until thawed.

until the dry ingredients are just incorporated.

4. Pinch off enough dough to form a 1-3/4-inch ball (about the size of a plum). Roll the dough lightly between the palms of your hands until it is round and smooth. Place on the parchment paper, spacing the cookies 2 inches apart. Crosshatch the cookies by pressing down on each ball with the tines of a fork in one direction and then the other until the cookies are 2 3/4 inches wide and 1/2 inch thick. **Bake for 8 - 10 minutes**, until the cookies are just set and beginning to brown. Slide the parchment onto cooling racks and don't try to move individual cookies until they are cool. They will seem underdone but will firm up as they cool.

VARIATIONS

Chocolate Chip Peanut Butter Cookies – at the end of mixing, stir in 1/2 to 1 cup of dairy-free chocolate chips.

Peanutty Peanut Butter Cookies – at the end of mixing, stir in 1/2 cup chopped peanuts.

My chocolate chip cookies have a little more flour, less salt, and a different mixing method than Toll House® cookies. This makes a cookie with more body and a sweet, rather than a salty, aftertaste. Using margarine instead of butter also makes for a thicker cookie.

Chocolate Chip Cookies

MAKES 30 COOKIES

2-1/3 cups all-purpose flour, fluffed, scooped
   and leveled into measuring cups
1 teaspoon baking soda
1/4 teaspoon salt

2 sticks (16 tablespoons) unsalted non-dairy
   stick margarine (such as Fleischmann's®),
   softened until pliable (about 15 minutes)
3/4 cup granulated sugar
3/4 cup packed light brown sugar
2 large eggs, room temperature
1 teaspoon vanilla extract

1-3/4 cups non-dairy chocolate chips
   (see page 15 for brands)
1 cup chopped pecans

1. Preheat the oven to 375 degrees F. with racks in the upper and lower thirds of the oven. Line 2 cookie sheets with kosher parchment paper (such as Reynolds®). Cut 2 more sheets of parchment to the same size and set them aside.

2. Sift together the flour, baking soda and salt. Set aside.

3. In a mixer bowl, beat the margarine, granulated sugar and brown sugar, on medium speed, until lightened in color and

These cookies are at their very best as soon as they cool with the chocolate chips still soft. They'll keep for one more day if well wrapped. They may be frozen in one layer, on a cookie sheet, and then transferred to a storage container or plastic bag. This way they won't freeze together and you'll be able to defrost at room temperature, or unwrap and microwave-defrost for 5 - 10 seconds, or until thawed.

texture (about 3 - 5 minutes). Beat in the eggs, one at a time and continue to beat for 1 minute until well blended. Beat in the vanilla.

4. Add the flour mixture all at once. Beat on low speed, or stir in by hand, just until the dry ingredients are incorporated. Stir in the chocolate chips and nuts.

5. Drop the dough by well-rounded tablespoonful onto the prepared cookie sheets, leaving 2 inches between mounds.

6. **Bake for 5 minutes.** Move the top cookie sheet to the lower rack, and the bottom sheet to the top. **Bake for 4 - 5 minutes** more until no beads of moisture can be seen on the surface of the cookies and the cookies are just barely firm. Slide the parchment paper onto cooling racks. Repeat with the remaining dough.

I adore these big, moist and fruity oatmeal cookies. With less oatmeal and a hint of vanilla and molasses, these cookies taste quite a bit different from commercial oatmeal cookies. Use spices to suit your taste.

Chewy Oatmeal Raisin Cookies

MAKES 9 LARGE COOKIES

1-1/8 cups all-purpose flour, fluffed, scooped
 and leveled into measuring cups
1/4 teaspoon baking soda
1/8 teaspoon salt
1/4 teaspoon cinnamon
1/2 cup old-fashioned rolled oats

1 stick (8 tablespoons) non-dairy unsalted
 margarine (such as Fleischmann's®),
 softened until pliable (about 15 minutes)
1/2 cup packed light brown sugar
1/4 cup granulated sugar
1 large egg, room temperature
1 teaspoon molasses
1 teaspoon vanilla extract

3/4 cup raisins
1/3 cup coarsely chopped walnuts

1. Preheat the oven to 325 degrees F. with a rack in the middle of the oven. Line a cookie sheet with kosher parchment paper (such as Reynolds®).

2. In a small bowl, mix together the flour, baking soda, salt, cinnamon and oats.

3. Place the margarine, brown sugar and granulated sugar in a large mixer bowl.

Oatmeal Raisin Cookies can be stored in a covered container for a few days. Freeze them, individually wrapped, for up to 3 months. Defrost wrapped cookies at room temperature, or unwrap and microwave-defrost until thawed.

Beat on medium speed until well mixed. Beat in the egg, molasses and vanilla extract just until incorporated. Add the flour mixture all at once. Stir, or beat on low, just until incorporated. Stir in the raisins and walnuts.

4. Using a 1/4-cup ice cream scoop, or a large spoon, drop the dough onto the prepared cookie sheet leaving 1 inch between each cookie. **Bake 18-22 minutes** until the cookies still glisten and look undercooked. If you are going to eat them that day, they can be baked 1 minute more. Slide the parchment paper onto a cooling rack. By the time you do this, the cookies will begin to look cooked and flattened.

BERRY
FRANGIPANE
TART
PAGE 179

ÉCLAIRS WITH VANILLA CUSTARD FILLING
PAGE 206

RASPBERRY AMARETTO LAYER CAKE
PAGE 142

SOUR CREEM
POUNDCAKE
PAGE 117

PECAN TOFFEE CHEEZECAKE
PAGE 63

CUPCAKES WITH SIMPLE VANILLA BUTTERCREEM FROSTING
PAGE 163

PISTACHIO
ICE CREEM
PAGE 42

HOT FUDGE
PAGE 210

GERMAN
CHOCOLATE CAKE
PAGE 127

INDIVIDUAL
TIRAMISU
PAGE 154

LEMON CURD
PHYLLO
TARTLETS
WITH BERRIES
PAGE 202

CARAMEL PEAR
PHYLLO CUP
PAGE 197

CHOCOLATE CREEM TART
PAGE 188

RICE PUDDING
PAGE 46

CAKES

This dark, rich and nutty cake is bursting with full chocolate flavor. The vanilla glaze provides perfect balance to the chocolate interior. It's easy to prepare, makes a nice presentation and serves a lot of people - a very nice party food. You can freeze it whole for future entertaining, or in individually wrapped slices, to enjoy throughout the week. It actually gets moister when frozen.

Chocolate Walnut Bundt Cake

SERVES 14 - 18

6 ounces non-dairy unsweetened chocolate (such as Hershey's®), finely chopped
3/4 cup plus 1 tablespoon oil
1-1/2 cups granulated sugar
1-1/4 cups packed light brown sugar
1 cup boiling water

1-1/2 cups sifted cake flour, spooned into measuring cups
1-1/2 teaspoons baking soda
1 teaspoon baking powder
1/2 teaspoon salt
1 cup all-purpose flour, fluffed, scooped and leveled into a measuring cup, reserve 1 tablespoon of flour
1-1/2 cups walnuts, finely chopped

1/2 cup Tofutti® Better Than Sour Cream, room temperature
4 large eggs, room temperature
2 teaspoons vanilla extract

Vanilla Glaze
1-2/3 cups powdered sugar
1 teaspoon vanilla extract
2 tablespoons plus 2 teaspoons Silk® soy creamer or non-dairy creamer, divided
1/4 stick (2 tablespoons) unsalted non-dairy margarine (such as Fleischmann's®)

Garnish (optional)
1 tablespoon finely chopped walnuts

Tips

To remove the cake from the pan without damaging the nonstick surface, I use a plastic tongue scraper (from the dentist), because it is very flexible and molds to the shape of the cake (alternatively use a flat wooden coffee stirrer). Don't forget to also loosen the cake at the center core.

1. Preheat the oven to 350 degrees F. with a rack in the lower third of the oven. Grease and flour a nonstick 12-cup Bundt pan.

2. Place the chocolate, oil, granulated and brown sugars, in a large microwave-safe bowl. Pour the boiling water over the chocolate mixture. Let stand for a minute and then stir. Microwave on medium-low power, in 15-second increments, until the chocolate is melted.

3. In a small bowl, sift together the cake flour, baking soda, baking powder, salt and all but 1 tablespoon of all-purpose flour. Mix the reserved tablespoon of flour with the walnuts, and set them aside.

4. In a small bowl, combine the sour cream substitute, eggs and vanilla. On medium-low, alternately beat the flour and egg mixtures into the chocolate mixture, starting and ending with flour. Stir in the floured walnuts.

5. Pour the batter into the prepared pan. Tap the pan on the counter to remove air bubbles. **Bake 55 – 60 minutes** until a tester comes out with no moist batter on it. Let the cake cool in the pan. Loosen the edges of the cake and then invert it onto a mesh cooling rack. Set the rack over a pan.

6. For the glaze, place the 2 tablespoons of soy creamer and the margarine into a small microwave-safe container. Micro-

Tips

The cake can be stored at room temperature or in the refrigerator, for up to 4 days. Wrap it in foil, or use a covered cake holder. Remove it from the refrigerator 30 minutes before serving, as it tastes best at room temperature.

The cake tastes even better after it has been frozen. Wrap it well in foil and keep it frozen for up to 3 months. To freeze slices, wrap each slice individually and then put the slices in a plastic bag. Leave wrapped, and defrost at room temperature, overnight. Individual slices can be unwrapped and defrosted on microwave-defrost for 15-30 seconds, until thawed.

wave on high, in 15 second increments, until the margarine is melted. Add the vanilla. Sift the powdered sugar into a small bowl. Whisk in the soy mixture. Whisk in as much of the reserved soy creamer as necessary to get a thick, but flowing, glaze. Pour the glaze over the cake and let it drip down the sides. Sprinkle the chopped walnuts on the wet glaze. Let the glaze set before wrapping the cake.

When you crave a simple piece of cake to go with a nice cup of coffee, this will make your heart soar. It's dense, sweet and so moist; perfect plain or as the foil for ice cream and hot fudge, or strawberries and whipped cream.

Sour Creem Poundcake

SERVES 10 - 12

1/2 cup Tofutti® Better Than Sour Cream, room temperature
3 tablespoons water, room temperature
3/4 teaspoon vanilla extract

2 cups sifted cake flour, spooned into measuring cups
1-1/3 cups sugar
1/8 teaspoon baking soda
1/4 teaspoon salt

1-1/4 sticks (10 tablespoons) unsalted non-dairy margarine (such as Fleischmann's®), softened until pliable (about 15 minutes), cut into tablespoon-size pieces

2 large eggs, room temperature
1 large egg yolk, room temperature

1. Preheat the oven to 350 degrees F. with a rack in the lower third of the oven. Grease and flour a 5 x 9-inch glass loaf pan.

2. In a medium bowl, whisk the sour cream substitute, water and vanilla.

3. Into a large mixer bowl place the flour, sugar, baking soda and salt. Beat on low, for a minute or two, to blend the ingredients.

The cake may be stored at room temperature for up to 3 days, if wrapped tightly in aluminum foil. For longer storage freeze the whole cake, wrapped tightly in foil, for up to 3 months. Wrap individual slices in plastic wrap and then place the slices in a plastic bag. Microwave-defrost 3/8-inch thick slices for 10 seconds, or thaw the entire loaf, still wrapped, overnight at room temperature.

4. Add the margarine and 3/4 of the Tofutti mixture to the flour mixture. Beat on low, until blended. Increase the speed to medium and beat for 2 minutes, until smooth and aerated.

5. Whisk the eggs and egg yolk into the remaining Tofutti mixture. Add this to the batter in three additions, beating on medium-low after each addition. Scrape down the bowl and beat until blended.

6. Spoon the batter into the pan, rap the pans sharply on the counter to remove any air pockets, and shake the pan to level the top. **Bake for 55 - 65 minutes** until a cake tester inserted at an angle, just off center, comes out barely clean (the center will have a lengthwise strip that will appear undercooked – do not insert the tester here). Let the cake cool in the pan. Run a knife around the perimeter of the pan and then invert it. Turn the cake right side up.

This typical "sour cream" coffeecake has a delicate texture and a sweet ribbon of chocolate pecan filling. Make sure to use finely chopped chocolate or mini-chips so that the filling doesn't fall to the bottom of the cake (enJoylife® chips are minis, although the package doesn't specify).

Chocolate Chip Pecan Loaf

SERVES 6 - 8

1 cup sifted cake flour, spooned into a measuring cup

1/2 cup all-purpose flour, fluffed, scooped and leveled into a measuring cup

1 teaspoon baking powder

1/8 teaspoon salt

1/2 teaspoon baking soda

3/4 cup granulated sugar

1 stick (8 tablespoons) unsalted non-dairy margarine (such as Fleischmann's®), softened until pliable (about 15 minutes), cut into tablespoon-size pieces

2 large eggs, room temperature

3/4 cup Tofutti® Better Than Sour Cream, room temperature, divided

1-1/2 teaspoons vanilla extract

Filling

1/2 cup walnuts or pecans, finely chopped

3 tablespoons packed light brown sugar

1/2 teaspoon cinnamon

1/2 cup enJoylife® semisweet chocolate chips (or bar chocolate, finely chopped)

A nice variation is to use currants in the filling instead of, or in addition to, the chocolate chips.

Crumb Topping
1/3 cup all-purpose flour, fluffed, scooped and leveled into a measuring cup
1/4 stick (2 tablespoons) unsalted non-dairy margarine, melted
Walnuts, brown sugar and cinnamon, reserved from above

1. Preheat the oven to 350 degrees F. with a rack in the middle of the oven. Grease and flour a 5 x 9-inch glass loaf pan.

2. In a large mixer bowl, mix together the flours, baking powder, salt, baking soda and sugar. Add the margarine, 1/2 cup sour cream substitute and the vanilla. Beat on low until blended. Increase the speed to medium, and beat for 2 minutes until smooth and aerated.

3. Whisk the eggs into the remaining sour cream substitute. Add this to the batter in three additions, beating on medium-low after each addition. Scrape down the bowl and beat until blended.

4. For the filling, mix together the pecans, brown sugar and cinnamon.

5. Spoon 1/2 of the batter into the pan. Sprinkle on 1/2 of the filling and then sprinkle on 1/4 cup of chocolate chips. Spoon on the remaining batter into an even layer. Sprinkle on the remaining 1/4 cup of chocolate chips.

6. For the topping, stir the flour into the remaining filling. Stir in the margarine.

The cake can be served when cooled, or wrapped in foil and stored for several days. It gets even moister by the second day.

For longer storage, freeze the whole cake wrapped tightly in foil, for up to 3 months. Wrap individual slices in plastic wrap and then place the slices in a plastic bag. Microwave-defrost 3/8-inch thick slices for 10 seconds, or thaw the entire loaf, still wrapped, overnight at room temperature.

Pinch the topping into small lumps and distribute them on top of the batter.

7. **Bake for 55 - 65 minutes** until a tester inserted into the center of the cake comes out with no crumbs attached.

8. Cool the cake on a wire rack, run a knife around the edges and then remove the cake from the pan. Let the cake cool completely before serving.

Lemon Poundcake

This poundcake has a great texture - neither too dense nor too light. The syrup gives it a sweet/tart outer edge and a very moist interior. If you prefer a bolder lemon taste, increase the lemon zest and substitute lemon juice for all or part of the soymilk.

SERVES 12 - 14
MAKE 1 DAY AHEAD

2 cups sifted cake flour, spooned into measuring cups
1/2 teaspoon baking powder
1/4 teaspoon baking soda
1/2 teaspoon salt

2 sticks (16 tablespoons) non-dairy unsalted margarine (such as Fleischmann's®), cold
1 cup sugar
4 large eggs, room temperature
4 tablespoons dairy-case soymilk (such as Silk®), room temperature
1 teaspoon vanilla extract
1 teaspoon lemon zest (the rind without any white attached)

Syrup
1/4 cup fresh lemon juice
1/4 cup sugar

1. Preheat the oven to 350 degrees F. with a rack in middle of the oven. Grease and flour a 5 x 9-inch glass loaf pan.

2. In a small bowl, mix together the flour, baking powder, baking soda and salt.

3. In a large mixer bowl, on medium-high speed, beat the margarine and 1 cup sugar until lightened in color and texture (5 - 7

Tips

When the cake is completely cool, wrap it in foil and let it stand at room temperature, overnight, before slicing.

The cake will stay moist and delicious for several days if well wrapped in foil. For longer storage freeze the whole cake, wrapped tightly in foil, for up to 3 months. Wrap individual slices in plastic wrap and then place the slices in a plastic bag. Microwave-defrost 3/8-inch thick slices for 10 seconds, or thaw the entire loaf, still wrapped, overnight at room temperature.

minutes). On low, beat in the eggs one at a time. Mix together the soy milk and vanilla. Beginning with the flour, alternately beat the flour mixture and the soy milk mixture into the batter, on low speed or by hand, until the dry ingredients are just incorporated and the mixture is smooth.

4. **Bake for 55 - 60 minutes** until a tester inserted into the cake comes out clean (the very top center will still be moist and might leave crumbs attached, so check to the side of the center crack).

5. While the cake is baking, place the lemon juice and 1/4 cup sugar in a small pot. Heat over medium heat until the sugar dissolves.

6. Remove the cake from the oven. Pierce the top of the cake all over with a skewer and then brush the top of the cake with the lemon syrup. Let cool for 10 minutes. Loosen the sides of the cake and invert it to remove the cake from the pan. Pierce the bottom of the cake and brush it with some of the syrup. Turn the cake right-side up. Brush the sides of the cake with some more syrup. Set the warm loaf on a cooling rack. Brush the remaining syrup over the top of the cake. Use all of the syrup, but make sure that it does not pool in the crack on the top of the cake or it will make a mushy spot in the finished cake.

This dark chocolate "buttermilk" layer cake is rich and light-textured. Buttermilk's tang is replicated by using balsamic vinegar, which unlike other vinegars, will leave no aftertaste. The combination of billowy frosting and light chocolate cake is outstanding.

Chocolate Marshmallow Layer Cake

SERVES 12

Chocolate "Buttermilk" Base Cake
1 cup sifted cake flour, spooned into a
    measuring cup
2/3 cup all-purpose flour, fluffed, scooped
    and leveled into measuring cups
1 teaspoon baking soda
1/4 teaspoon salt

3 ounces non-dairy semisweet chocolate,
    finely chopped (see page 15 for brands)
1/3 cup boiling water

1-1/4 sticks (10 tablespoons) non-dairy
    margarine (such as Fleischmann's®), cold

1-1/3 cups sugar, divided
3 large eggs, room temperature and
    separated
1 teaspoon vanilla extract

1/3 cup Tofutti® Better Than Sour Cream,
    mixed with 2/3 cup water and 1 teaspoon
    balsamic vinegar

Tips

Egg whites will not whip if there is any trace of grease present. For extra precaution, you can wipe down the bowl and beaters with vinegar.

If you overbeat the egg whites so that they are stiff and dry, the cake will not rise properly. You'll know if you have over-beaten them because they'll ball up and look like little bits of Styrofoam when you try to fold them into your batter. If this happens, add another egg white into the beaten egg whites, and beat briefly to combine. Continue to fold the egg whites into the batter using all but 1/2 cup of them (to account for the extra egg white that you added).

Chocolate Marshmallow Frosting

3 sticks (24 tablespoons) unsalted non-dairy margarine (such as Fleischmann's®), softened at room temperature for 15 minutes

2 cups chopped non-dairy semisweet chocolate

1 pound jar Marshmallow Fluff®

1 teaspoon vanilla extract

1. Preheat the oven to 350 degrees F. with a rack in the middle of the oven. Grease two 9-inch round cake pans. Line the pans with kosher parchment paper (such as Reynolds®), grease the paper and then flour the pans.

2. Sift together the flours, baking soda and salt. Set aside.

3. Place the chocolate in a small microwave-safe bowl. Pour the boiling water over the chocolate. Set aside for a minute and then stir. If the chocolate isn't completely melted, microwave on medium power, in 30 seconds increments, until the chocolate melts. Set aside to cool.

4. In a large bowl, beat the margarine and all but 1 tablespoon of the sugar until light and fluffy (about 5 - 7 minutes). Beat in the egg yolks one at a time. Blend in the melted chocolate mixture and the vanilla.

5. On low, beat in the flour mixture alternately with the non-dairy sour cream mixture, beating just until incorporated.

Cakes • 125

Because Chocolate Marshmallow Cake has a moist filling, it needs to be stored in a covered cake-holder in the refrigerator. Remove the cake from the refrigerator 1 hour before serving to bring out the flavors.

The unfrosted cake layers can be made ahead and stored, well-wrapped in foil, for 1 day. For longer storage, freeze the cakes, wrapped tightly in foil. Leave the cakes in their wrapping, and defrost at room temperature, overnight.

6. In a large grease-free mixer bowl, beat the egg whites, using grease-free beaters, until soft peaks just start to form. Beat in the remaining 1 tablespoon of sugar and continue to beat until stiff peaks form. Stir 1/3 of the whites into the batter and then fold in the remaining whites until no streaks remain.

7. Divide the batter between the two pre-pared pans. Bake for 25 - 30 minutes, or until a toothpick inserted into the center of the cake comes out clean, with no crumbs attached. Cool the cakes in the pans. Run a knife around the perimeter of the cakes to loosen the edges. Invert the pans onto cake boards, remove the parchment paper, place cake boards on the cakes and then re-invert so the cakes are right-side-up.

8. Place the chocolate in a microwave-safe bowl. Heat on medium power for 2 minutes. Stir and heat for another minute or until the chocolate is melted and smooth when stirred. Set it aside to cool.

9. In a large mixer bowl, beat the margarine until softened and smooth. Beat in the Fluff until thoroughly combined. Beat in the chocolate and vanilla, until blended.

10. To assemble the cake, spread one layer with 1/2-inch of frosting, top with the second cake, and frost the cake all over.

This wonderful chocolate "sour cream" layer cake is fine-textured but a bit firmer than the Chocolate "Buttermilk" Base Cake, from the previous recipe. A traditional filling for German Chocolate Cake would have butter and evaporated milk or cream. By substituting coconut milk (a non-dairy product), the filling has the right texture and is actually more flavorful.

German Chocolate Cake

SERVES 12

Chocolate Sour Creem Base Cake
1 cup dairy-case soymilk (such as Silk®),
    room temperature, divided
5 ounces non-dairy semisweet chocolate,
    (see page 15, for brands) finely chopped

1 cup sifted cake flour, spooned into a
    measuring cup
1 cup all-purpose flour, fluffed, scooped and
    leveled into a measuring cup
1/4 cup unsweetened cocoa powder
    (not Dutch processed)
1-1/2 teaspoons baking soda
1/4 teaspoon salt

1 stick (8 tablespoons) unsalted non-dairy
    margarine (such as Fleischmann's®),
    softened until pliable (about 15 minutes)
2 tablespoons oil
1-1/4 cups granulated sugar
1/2 cup packed light brown sugar

2 large eggs, room temperature
1 teaspoon vanilla extract
3/4 cup Tofutti® Better Than Sour Cream, room
    temperature

(continued)

To prevent the cakes from rising unevenly, you can wrap the pans with cake strips (www.bakerscatalogue.com, item #7262). Otherwise, the tops of the cakes will be rounded, and will need to be trimmed so that the two layers mate nicely.

Coconut Pecan Filling
4 large egg yolks
1-1/2 cups coconut milk
  (for kosher brands, see page 19)
1-1/2 cups sugar
3/4 stick (6 tablespoons) unsalted non-dairy margarine (preferably Fleishmann's®), cut into chunks

1/2 teaspoon vanilla extract
2 cups sweetened coconut flakes
  (see pg 27, for kosher brands)
2 cups chopped pecans

Garnish (optional)
3/4 cup pecan quarters
1 ounce non-dairy semisweet chocolate, finely chopped
1/2 teaspoon oil

1. Preheat the oven to 350 degrees F. with an oven rack in the middle of the oven. Grease two 9-inch round cake pans and line them with kosher parchment paper (such as Reynolds®). Grease the parchment and flour the pans.

2. For the cakes, place 1/4 cup soymilk in a microwave-safe container and microwave on high until very hot. Add the chopped chocolate and swirl it so the chocolate is covered with the liquid. Let stand a minute, and then stir. If the chocolate is not completely melted, microwave it on medium, in 30 second increments, until melted. Set aside to cool.

To get the cakes out of the pans, run a knife around the perimeter of the cakes to loosen the edges. Invert the pans onto cardboard cake boards, remove the parchment paper, top with another cake board and re-invert so the cakes are right-side-up.

3. Sift together the flours, cocoa, baking soda and salt.

4. In a large mixer bowl, beat the margarine until creamy. Add the oil, granulated sugar and brown sugar. Beat for 3 - 5 minutes until well mixed and aerated. Beat in the eggs, one at a time, until blended and then continue to beat for 1 minute. Beat in the vanilla, sour cream substitute and the chocolate mixture, until blended.

5. On low, alternately beat in the flour mixture and the remaining 3/4 cup soymilk, adding the soymilk in a slow stream so that the batter doesn't "curdle". The batter will be very thick, like chocolate mousse. Divide the batter between the pans. Shake the pans back and forth to get the batter to level out and then rap the pans sharply on the counter to get rid of air pockets. **Bake for 25 - 30 minutes** until a tester comes out clean, with no moist crumbs attached. Cool the cakes, in the pans, on a wire rack. Remove the cakes from the pans (see sidebar).

6. For the filling, whisk the egg yolks lightly, in a medium nonstick saucepan. Gradually whisk in the coconut milk and sugar. Add the margarine. Cook the mixture over moderate heat, stirring constantly, until just steaming. (The temperature will be 170 - 175 degrees F. on an instant-read thermometer.) Do not let it boil. Strain the mixture into a storage container. It will be fairly thin, and very yellow, but will

Cakes • 129

The unfrosted layers can be wrapped in foil and stored at room temperature overnight, or they may be frozen for 3 months. Defrost them, in their wrapping, overnight at room temperature.

The finished cake can be stored in a covered cake-holder, in the refrigerator, for up to 3 days. Remove the cake from the refrigerator 1 hour before serving.

thicken and turn whiter as it cools. Stir in the vanilla, coconut, and pecans. Place it in the refrigerator to cool completely, stirring occasionally. The filling can be made several days ahead.

7. To assemble the cake, spread half of the filling over the top of the cake to within 1/4-inch of the edge. Place the second layer on top of the filling. Arrange the quartered pecans around the edge of the cake, placing them at a slight angle and overlapping them a little. Place the second layer on top. Spoon the remaining filling onto the cake to within 1/4-inch of the edge. Place quartered pecans along the edge, as above (you'll get an effect that looks like a fluted pie crust). Spread the filling, lightly, to meet the pecans.

8. For the finishing touch, combine the semisweet chocolate and the oil in a microwave-safe bowl. Heat on medium, in 15-second increments, until the chocolate is melted and smooth. Transfer the chocolate mixture to a small parchment cone, snip the tip and drizzle chocolate over the top of the cake (or drizzle it onto the cake using fork tines).

Carrot Cake

If you've had problems with inconsistency in your carrot cake, it's probably because the amount of carrot used will vary unless you weigh the trimmed carrots and then grate them. Packing the carrots into the cup will help with consistency, too. If you've tried non-dairy cream cheese frosting before and had failures, give this one a try. There's a secret to making it come out great.

2 cups all-purpose flour, fluffed, scooped and leveled into measuring cups
1 teaspoon cinnamon
1 teaspoon baking soda
1 teaspoon baking powder
1/2 teaspoon salt
1 cup walnuts, coarsely chopped
1 cup raisins

1-1/4 cups oil
1/2 cup firmly packed light brown sugar
1-1/2 cups granulated sugar
4 large eggs, room temperature

3 cups packed grated carrots (1 pound trimmed carrots, about 4 - 10 untrimmed)

Creem Cheese Frosting
1-1/4 sticks (10 tablespoons) unsalted non-dairy margarine, softened until pliable (about 15 minutes)
16 ounces Tofutti® Better than Cream Cheese, at cool room temperature
1 teaspoon vanilla extract
2 cups powdered sugar

Garnish (optional)
1 cup finely chopped walnuts

To get the cakes out of the pans, run a knife around the perimeter of the cakes to loosen the edges. Invert the pans onto cardboard cake boards, remove the parchment paper, top with another cake board and re-invert so the cakes are right-side-up.

Unfrosted cake layers can be frozen for 3 months. Frosted carrot cake will keep several days in the refrigerator, in a covered cake holder. Do not freeze the frosted cake.

1. Preheat the oven to 350 degrees F. with a rack in the middle of the oven. Grease two 9-inch round cake pans. Line the pans with kosher parchment paper (such as Reynolds®). Grease the paper and flour the pans.

2. In a small bowl, mix together the flour, cinnamon, baking soda, baking powder and salt. Stir in the walnuts and raisins.

3. In a large mixer bowl, beat together the oil and sugars. Beat in the eggs, one at a time, until well blended and smooth. In three additions, stir in the flour mixture. Stir in the carrots. Divide the mixture between the two pans and rap them on the counter to remove air pockets. **Bake for 35 - 40 minutes** until a tester comes out clean, with no moist crumbs attached. Cool cakes on a cooling rack. Remove cakes from pans (see sidebar).

4. For the frosting; in a large mixer bowl, beat the margarine until creamy. The secret to making this frosting work, is to blend the margarine and cream cheese substitute using a wooden spoon. DO NOT BEAT IT or the mixture will thin and become sauce! Stir in the vanilla. Stir in the powdered sugar one-third at a time.

5. Place one cake (on its board) on a turntable or counter. Spread frosting on the top of the cake to make a 1/4-inch layer. Remove the second cake from its board and place it on the frosting. Spread frosting onto the sides of the cake. Swirl the remaining frosting onto the top of the cake, or pipe stars across the top. Press the walnuts into the sides of the cake.

I love applesauce cake because it's so moist and spicy. It keeps for several days and is a nice snack cake or casual dessert for a crowd.

Applesauce Honey Cake

SERVES 15 - 25

2 cups all-purpose flour, fluffed, scooped and
   leveled into measuring cups
2 teaspoons baking soda
1 teaspoon salt
1 teaspoon cinnamon
1/2 teaspoon nutmeg
1/4 teaspoon ground cloves
1/4 teaspoon allspice

4 large eggs, room temperature
1 cup oil
1/2 cup sugar
1 cup honey
1 tablespoon molasses

2 cups applesauce
1 cup raisins
1 cup coarsely chopped walnuts
1 tablespoon all-purpose flour

Garnish (optional)
Powdered sugar or 1/2 recipe Creem Cheese
   Frosting (page 131)

1. Preheat the oven to 350 degrees F. with a rack in the middle of the oven. Grease a 9 x 12-inch baking pan. Line the pan with

The cake can be removed from the pan whole by inverting it onto a board and then re-inverting it or you can cut it into squares and remove them individually.

This cake is very moist and will keep for several days. Refrigerate, and loosely cover or place in a covered cake-holder. It tastes best when left at room temperature for 15 minutes before serving. Do not freeze the frosted cake.

kosher parchment paper (such as Reynolds®) and grease the paper.

2. Into a small bowl, sift together 2 cups flour, baking soda, salt, cinnamon, nutmeg, cloves and allspice.

3. In a large mixer bowl, whisk together the eggs and oil. On low, beat in the sugar, honey and molasses.

4. On low, alternately beat the flour mixture and applesauce into the batter. Mix the raisins and nuts with the 1 tablespoon of flour and stir them into the batter.

5. Pour the batter into the prepared pan. **Bake for 45 minutes** until a tester inserted into the center of the cake comes out clean, with no moist crumbs attached. Cool the cake, in the pan, on a cooling rack.

6. Serve the cake either dusted with powdered sugar or piped with Creem Cheese Frosting.

In this cake, an airy sponge cake complements a fluffy, dark chocolate mousse filling. Make the cake 1 day ahead so that the mousse will set and the cake can be cut into neat slices.

Chocolate Mousse Cake

SERVES 10

Classic Genoise (Buttery Sponge Cake)
1-1/2 tablespoons unsalted non-dairy
    margarine (such as Fleischmann's®)
1-1/2 tablespoons vegetable oil
4 large eggs
6 tablespoons sugar
1 cup sifted cake flour, spooned into a
    measuring cup

Simple Syrup
1/3 cup sugar
1/3 cup water
3 tablespoons rum (or liqueur of choice)

Chocolate Mousse
4 large pasteurized eggs (for regular eggs,
    directions follow)
1/3 cup sugar
12 ounces non-dairy, semisweet chocolate,
    finely chopped
2 eight-ounce cartons Richwhip®, thawed
    and divided

Garnish (optional)
Chocolate curls or shavings

1. Preheat the oven to 375 degrees F with a rack in the middle of the oven. Grease two 9-inch round cake pans, line with kosher parchment paper (such as Reynolds®), grease the paper and then flour the pans.

2. In a medium microwave-safe bowl, melt the margarine with the oil. Set aside.

3. In a metal mixer bowl, lightly whisk the eggs and the sugar. Place over simmering water and whisk 1 - 2 minutes until warm (about 110 degrees F.).

4. Remove the bowl from the heat and beat the mixture, with an electric mixer on high, until tripled in volume and very thick, about 5 minutes.

5. Sift 1/2 of the flour over the eggs and gently fold together. Repeat with the remaining flour.

6. Remove about 1/2 cup egg mixture and stir it thoroughly into the margarine-oil mixture. Fold this back into the egg mixture. Divide the batter between the two prepared pans. Do not tap the pans.

7. **Bake for 7 - 9 minutes** until the edges start to pull away from the sides of the pan and the top is glossy and slightly springy. Cool the cakes in the pans. Remove the cakes from the pans (see sidebar). Wrap the cakes in aluminum foil and set aside until ready to use.

Baking Serving and Storing Tips

If you are using regular eggs, combine the eggs, sugar and 1/4 cup water in a shallow metal bowl. Simmer 1-inch of water in a skillet. Have a rubber scraper, instant-read thermometer, a timer and a large mixer bowl near the stove. Place the shallow bowl into the simmering water and cook the egg mixture to 160 degrees F. (30 – 60 seconds), rapidly stirring with a rubber scraper and checking the temperature every 15 seconds. Transfer the mixture to a large mixer bowl and continue with the recipe.

8. For the simple syrup, combine the sugar, water and rum in a small saucepan. Heat over medium heat until the sugar melts. Set aside.

9. For the mousse, place the chocolate into the top of a double-boiler and set it over hot, but not simmering, water. Let the chocolate melt, stirring often. Remove the pot from over the water and let it cool until just barely warm.

10. Break the eggs into a large mixer bowl and whisk in the sugar. Beat the mixture on high until thick, like softly whipped cream (about 5 - 10 minutes). Fold in the melted chocolate.

11. Pour one carton of Richwhip® into a cold mixer bowl. Beat on high until the topping forms soft peaks. Fold this into the chocolate mixture.

12. Assemble the cake in either an 8 or a 9-inch springform pan, depending on how much your cakes have shrunk. Check the size of both layers before starting to assemble the cake. There should be no space between the cake and the pan sides. If necessary, use the 8-inch pan and cut the cakes to fit. If you are taking the cake somewhere, you can replace the bottom of the springform with a cardboard cake round. Place one cake layer in the pan, bottom side up. Using a pastry brush, pat on the simple syrup, using about half of

To pipe shells, place a star tip into a decorating bag and fill the bag with the whipped Richwhip®. Hold the bag at a 45 degree angle, with the tip slightly above the surface of the cake.

Squeeze the bag, and lift the tip up a little as the shell forms.

Relax the pressure on the bag slightly and pull the bag down closer to the surface to form the tail of the shell.

Stop squeezing, and pull the tip away. Start each new shell at the tail of the previous shell.

Piping a shell.

the syrup. The cake should be moistened, but not drenched with syrup. Spoon on half of the chocolate mousse. Place the second cake layer on the mousse. Press down on the cake to make sure that it's level. Pat the remaining syrup onto the cake. Spoon on the remaining mousse. It will mound up over the top of the pan. Decoratively swirl the mousse so that it looks nice. Place the cake in a covered cake-holder, or cover it with a domed lid and refrigerate overnight.

13. Just before serving, dampen a knife and run it around the perimeter of the cake. Remove the springform sides and set the cake on a serving platter. Whip the second container of Richwhip® to stiff peaks. Pipe a simple shell border around the top of the cake and then sprinkle on the shavings in the center. An alternate decoration is to swirl on a layer of the whipped topping, and then garnish with the chocolate. Serve cold.

Sometimes this is called strawberry shortcake, although it has sponge-cake instead of a biscuit base. I've used a rich, dense genoise so that the cake will not get soggy when layered with the very moist strawberry filling.

Strawberry Creem Layer Cake

SERVES 8 - 10

Firm Genoise
3/8 stick (3 tablespoons) unsalted non-dairy stick margarine (such as Fleischmann's®)
1-1/2 tablespoons oil

6 large eggs
1/2 cup plus 1 tablespoon sugar

1 cup all-purpose flour, fluffed, scooped and leveled into a measuring cup
1/3 cup sifted cake flour, spooned into a measuring cup

Strawberry Filling
3 pounds strawberries (3 quarts)
2/3 cup sugar
1 tablespoon cornstarch
1 eight-ounce container Richwhip®, thawed
1 tablespoon powdered sugar, optional
1 packet Oetker Whiplt®, optional

1. Preheat the oven to 350 degrees F. Grease two 9-inch round cake pans, line with kosher parchment paper (such as Reynolds®), grease the paper and then flour the pans.

2. Place the margarine and oil in a micro-wave-safe bowl and heat on medium

To get the cakes out of the pans, invert the pans onto cardboard cake boards, remove the parchment paper, top with another cake board and re-invert so the cakes are right-side-up.

The cakes can be used immediately, wrapped in foil and stored at room temperature for 2 days, or can be frozen for 3 months. Thaw for a few hours before using.

power, until the margarine is melted. Set aside.

3. In a metal mixer bowl, lightly whisk together the eggs and the sugar. Place over a saucepan of simmering water and whisk 1 - 2 minutes until warm (about 110 degrees F.).

4. Remove the bowl from the heat and beat with an electric mixer, on high, until tripled in volume and very thick, about 5 minutes.

5. Mix together the flours. Sift 1/2 of the flour over the eggs and gently fold together. Repeat with the remaining flour.

6. Remove about 1/2 cup batter and stir it thoroughly into the margarine-oil mixture. Fold this into the remaining batter. Divide the batter between the two prepared pans. Do not tap the pans.

7. **Bake for 7 - 9 minutes** until the edges start to pull away from the sides of the pan, and the top is glossy and slightly springy. Run a knife around the edges of the pans to release the cakes, but leave the cakes in the pans until cool (see sidebar for removal).

8. At least 4 hours before serving, wash, hull and slice 3 cups of berries. Place them in a small pot and stir in the sugar. Let them stand for 15 - 30 minutes until the berries start exuding juice.

9. Place the cornstarch in a small bowl and stir in 2 tablespoons of the strawberry juice. Place the pot of berries on the stove and cook over medium-high heat

Tips

The cake tastes best if allowed to mellow in the refrigerator for a few hours. By the second day, fresh, local berries may have started to ferment. If non-local berries are used, they should still be fine by the second day. If you've spread Richwhip over the entire top of the cake, you can set a starburst of berries in the middle of the cake to make the cake look more festive.

Do not freeze the finished cake.

until the berries start to simmer. Stir in the cornstarch mixture. Simmer, stirring constantly, until the mixture becomes clear and bright. Remove the pot from the stove. If the berries you are using are not fully ripe and "in season", wash, hull and slice 3 cups of berries, and add to the hot berry mixture. Refrigerate until cold. Alternatively, if the berries are fresh, fully ripe berries, let the cooked mixture cool. Cover and refrigerate it. When ready to use, wash, hull and slice another 3 cups of berries, tip to stem, into 1/4-inch slices. Stir the fresh berries into the cold berry sauce.

10. If you plan to make the cake more than 4 hours ahead, use the WhipIt, to prevent the Richwhip from watering out. Combine it with the Richwhip and the powdered sugar, if using, in a large mixer bowl. Beat on medium-high to high, to stiff peaks.

11. For a quick, homey presentation, simply layer the cakes, filling and Richwhip. For a more polished presentation, arrange a row of the fresh cut berries around the perimeter of the cake with the tips facing outward. Spoon on half of the berry filling. Spoon or pipe on 2/3 of the Richwhip®. Put the second layer on top of the cake. Place a row of berries around the perimeter and fill the center with the remaining strawberry filling. Pipe the Richwhip® decoratively over the cake (I like to do a lattice design). If you do not have a decorating bag, spoon on the Richwhip but don't go all the way to the edge so that the perimeter of berries is showing.

The raspberry filling in this cake has a bright, fresh taste that really pops with flavor. The amaretto is subtle and a great compliment to the tartness of the filling. The cake works nicely for special occasions - a very sophisticated birthday or anniversary cake, for example. For a simpler version, see the directions at the end of the recipe.

Raspberry Amaretto Layer Cake

SERVES 10 - 12
MUST BE PREPARED 2 DAYS AHEAD

Raspberry Filling
1 twelve-ounce package frozen raspberries, thawed
3/4 cup sugar
1 tablespoon Surejell® Fruit Pectin for lower sugar recipes
1/4 cup water

Amaretto Simple Syrup
1/3 cup sugar
1/3 cup water
2 tablespoons amaretto liqueur (if kosher, use Amaretto di Saronno®)

Light Genoise Cake
3 tablespoons unsalted non-dairy stick margarine (such as Fleischmann's®)
1 tablespoon canola oil
5 large eggs
2/3 cup sugar
1-1/4 cups sifted cake flour, spooned into measuring cups

Raspberry filling can be made ahead and stored in the refrigerator for up to 5 days. Do not freeze.

The syrup can be used as soon as it is cool or stored in a covered container in the refrigerator for up to 3 weeks. Use at room temperature.

Amaretto Meringue Buttercreem

4 large pasteurized egg whites (*if using regular eggs, directions follow)

1-1/2 cups sugar

2 tablespoons water

2 sticks (16 tablespoons) unsalted non-dairy margarine

1 tablespoon amaretto liqueur

3/4 teaspoon pure almond extract

Garnish (optional)

1/2 cup sliced almonds, toasted until fragrant (about 3 minutes)

1. For the raspberry filling, thaw the raspberries in a food mill or medium mesh strainer, placed over a bowl. Press through to remove the raspberry seeds. Place the sugar in a 3 quart saucepan. Stir in the pectin. Add the water. Bring the mixture to a boil over medium-high heat. Stirring constantly, boil for 1 minute (don't start counting until after bubbles appear over the entire surface of the sugar syrup). Remove from the heat and stir in the sieved raspberries. Transfer the filling to a storage container. Cool, cover and refrigerate overnight or up to 5 days.

2. For the amaretto syrup, place the sugar and water in a small saucepan. Bring to a simmer over medium-high heat. Remove from the heat and stir in the amaretto.

3. For the cake, preheat the oven to 375 degrees F. with a rack in the middle of the

To remove the cakes from the pans, run a knife around the perimeter of the cakes to loosen the edges. Invert the pans onto cardboard cake boards, remove the parchment paper, top with another cake board and re-invert so the cakes are right-side-up. The cakes can be used immediately, wrapped in foil and stored at room temperature for 2 days, or can be frozen for 3 months. Thaw for a few hours before using.

oven. Grease two 9-inch round cake pans, line with kosher parchment paper (such as Reynolds®), grease the paper and then flour the pans.

4. Place the margarine and oil in a small microwave-safe bowl. Cover and microwave on high for 1 minute or until the margarine is melted and warm. Set aside.

5. Simmer about 2 inches water in a medium pot. In a metal mixer bowl, whisk together the eggs and sugar. Place the bowl over the simmering water and whisk the egg mixture 1 - 2 minutes until they are quite warm but not hot (about 110-120 degrees F.). Remove from the heat and beat the egg mixture on high, until the eggs have tripled in volume and are very thick, like softly whipped cream, about 5 minutes.

6. Sift half of the flour over the egg mixture and gently fold together. Repeat with the remaining flour. Remove 1 cup batter and stir this into the melted margarine. Pour this into the remaining batter and gently fold together. Divide the batter between the two pans. Do not tap the pans or the cakes will not rise. **Bake for 13 - 15 minutes** until the cakes are springy and pulling away from the sides of the pan. Cool the cakes in the pans and then remove them from the pans (see sidebar).

7. For the frosting, remove the margarine from the refrigerator so it can soften while you prepare the eggs.

Tips

For regular eggs, whisk together the eggs, sugar and water in a shallow metal bowl. Simmer 1-inch of water in a skillet. Have a rubber scraper, instant-read thermometer, a timer and a large mixer bowl near the stove. Place the bowl in the simmering water and cook the egg mixture to 160 degrees F. (30 – 60 seconds), rapidly stirring with a rubber scraper and checking the temperature every 15 seconds. Transfer the mixture to a large mixer bowl and continue with the recipe.

To work with refrigerated buttercreem, bring it to room temperature and then beat until fluffy.

8. Re-simmer the water in the pot. Thoroughly clean the mixer bowl, washing it down with vinegar to get rid of grease. Place the egg whites into the clean mixer bowl. Whisk in the water and sugar. Place the bowl over the simmering water and whisk constantly until the mixture reaches 120 - 130 degrees F. (1 - 3 minutes). The mixture will be very warm and the sugar granules should have dissolved. Remove the bowl from over the water. If you see any undissolved sugar crystals in the bowl, wipe these off with a paper towel. Beat the egg white mixture, on medium-high to high speed, until the mixture looks like thick shaving cream and the egg whites and bowl are cool (about 10 minutes). This is most easily done with a standing mixer using a balloon whisk attachment. To hasten the process, the bowl of eggs can be placed into a large bowl of ice water as you beat them.

9. Place 1-3/4 sticks of margarine into another large mixer bowl and beat until creamy. On low, beat in the whipped egg whites, a third at a time. Increase the mixer speed to medium-high and beat for 10 minutes. Add the remaining margarine and continue to beat until the mixture curdles and then smoothes out into a thick and creamy frosting (3-5 minutes). If after 5 minutes this has not happened, place the bowl in the refrigerator for 5 minutes, and then beat as above. Beat in the amaretto and almond extract.

Baking Serving and Storing Tips

All desserts made with buttercream taste best if the frosting is allowed to soften before eating. Frostings made with butter will take longer to soften than those made with margarine. Leave the cake at room temperature for 30-60 minutes before eating and the buttercreem should be smooth and soft but still firm enough to maintain its shape.

10. To assemble the cake: Leave the bottom layer on the cake board. Pierce the cake all over with a skewer. Dab on some of the syrup, making two passes over the cake. Fit a pastry bag with a medium star tip. Fill the pastry bag with 1/3 of the buttercream. Pipe a thin ring of buttercream around the perimeter of the top of the cake to contain the raspberry filling. Fill the center with a 1/16-inch layer of raspberry filling. Reserve the remaining filling. Pipe a 1/4- inch layer of buttercreem over the raspberry filling. Place the second layer on top of the frosted cake. Pierce the second cake all over with a skewer. Dab on some of the syrup, making two passes (you may have some syrup left over).

11. Lightly crush the toasted almonds. Spread the sides of the cake with frosting. Slide a spatula under the cake board and lift the cake up so that you can hold the board in one hand. With your other hand, pat the toasted almonds onto the sides of the cake. Set the cake back down on the work surface.

12. Spread a 1/16-inch layer of raspberry filling on the top of the cake to within 1/8 - 1/4 inch of the perimeter. On this perimeter, pipe a border to meet the raspberry filling and the frosted sides. Pipe lines, or a grid of buttercreem across the filling. Refrigerate the cake at least overnight or up to 2 days before serving. Let the cake stand at room temperature for 1 hour before serving to allow the buttercream to come to room temperature.

The cake can be stored for 4 days in the refrigerator, in a covered cake-holder. The buttercream version can be frozen for 3 months, but the raspberry filling loses some of its zing. Let the cake freeze before wrapping it in foil. To defrost, loosen the foil, or transfer the cake to a covered cake-holder. Defrost in the refrigerator, overnight. Let the cake stand at room temperature for 1 hour before serving.

VARIATIONS

Easier Raspberry Amaretto Layer Cake
Use the Simple Vanilla Buttercreem, on page 163, instead of the Meringue Buttercreem.

Raspberry Creem Cake
Delete the buttercreem and use 2 cartons of Richwhip®, thawed and then whipped with almond extract, and 1 tablespoon powdered sugar. You can also mix some of the raspberry filling into the whipped topping if you want to have a pink cake. Garnish with fresh raspberries, if desired. If you plan to make the cake ahead, consider using Oetker WhipIt®, so that the Richwhip does not get watery.

Birthday Cake
If you want to write on the cake, leave off the raspberry filling from the top of the cake, and spread the top with frosting, instead.

This wonderful cake has an easy chocolate frosting and a very rich, buttery sponge cake. It has more margarine and sugar than some of the other genoise I use, which makes it less airy – more like a traditional butter cake. For perfection, though, it still needs to have some syrup brushed onto it.

Light Chocolate or Mocha Layer Cake

SERVES 10 - 12

Rich Genoise
6 large eggs
3/4 cup plus 2 tablespoons sugar
1 cup all-purpose flour, fluffed, scooped and leveled into measuring cups
1/4 cup sifted cake flour, spooned into a measuring cup
1 stick (8 tablespoons) unsalted non-dairy margarine (such as Fleischmann's®), melted

Simple Syrup
1/4 cup sugar
1/4 cup water
2 tablespoons Kahlúa (for kosher alternative, see page 28)

Light Chocolate or Mocha Frosting
8 ounces non-dairy semisweet chocolate (see page 15, for brands), finely chopped
2-3/4 sticks (22 tablespoons) unsalted non-dairy margarine, room temperature, divided
2 cups powdered sugar, sifted
1 eight-ounce container Richwhip ®, thawed
2 teaspoons instant coffee powder, mixed with 2 teaspoons hot water and then cooled

Tips

To remove the cakes from the pans, invert them onto cardboard cake boards and remove the parchment paper. Leave the cakes upside down. The unfrosted cakes can be used immediately, or wrapped in foil and stored at room temperature for 2 days, or can be frozen for 3 months. Thaw for a few hours before frosting. Cakes that have been at room temperature for more than a day, may need more syrup than fresh cakes.

1. Preheat the oven to 375 degrees F. with a rack in the middle of the oven. Grease two 9-inch round cake pans and line with kosher parchment paper (such as Reynolds®). Grease and flour the pans and the parchment paper.

2. Place 1 stick margarine in a microwave-safe bowl. Cover and microwave on high for about 1 minute to melt the margarine. Set aside.

3. Simmer about 2 inches water in a medium pot. In a metal mixer bowl, whisk together the eggs and sugar. Place the bowl over the simmering water and whisk the egg mixture 1 - 2 minutes until quite warm but not hot (about 110-120 degrees F.). Remove from the heat, and beat the egg mixture on high, until the eggs have tripled in volume and are very thick, like softly whipped cream (about 5 minutes).

4. Sift together the flours. Sift 1/2 of the flour over the eggs and gently fold together. Repeat with the remaining flour.

5. Remove about 2 cups batter and stir thoroughly into the warm margarine. Fold this back into the remaining batter. Divide the batter between the two prepared pans. Do not tap the pans or the cakes will fall.

6. **Bake for 20 - 25 minutes** until the edges start to pull away from the sides of the pan and the top is glossy and slightly springy. Run a knife around the edges of the pans to release the cakes, but don't remove them from the pans until cool (see sidebar for removal).

Tips

The syrup can be made up to 3 weeks ahead (keep in the refrigerator, but bring to room temperature before using).

The frosted cake may be stored, in a cake-holder, in the refrigerator for up to 3 days. Let the cake stand at room temperature about 1 hour before serving.

The cake may be frozen whole, and then wrapped well in foil. To defrost, loosen the foil, or transfer the cake to a covered cake-holder. Defrost in the refrigerator, overnight.

7. For the syrup, combine the sugar and water in a small pot. Heat the mixture over medium heat until the sugar dissolves and then raise the heat, and bring the mixture to a simmer. Stir in the liqueur (if you want the flavor, but not the alcohol, add the liqueur before bringing the mixture to a boil). Let cool before using.

8. For the frosting, place the chocolate and 5 tablespoons margarine in the top of the double boiler. Set it over hot, but not simmering water, and let the chocolate and margarine melt, stirring occasionally. Remove from the heat and let the mixture cool.

9. Place the remaining margarine and the powdered sugar in a large mixer bowl. Beat for 5 - 7 minutes until light and fluffy. If making mocha frosting, beat in the coffee-water. Beat in the cooled chocolate.

10. Place the Richwhip® in another mixer bowl. Beat on high speed until the topping forms stiff peaks. Fold the whipped topping into the frosting and then whisk the frosting until well blended and fluffy.

11. To assemble the cake, poke holes all over the top of the cake with a small skewer. Brush the cake with the soaking syrup, using about half of the syrup. Spread on about 3/8-inch thick layer of frosting. Top with the second cake layer. Poke holes in that layer and brush the cake with more of the syrup. Spread frosting onto the sides of the cake, and then the top. Pipe on decorations as desired. Refrigerate until ready to serve.

This is a great all-occasion layer cake. The two-stage mixing method is easier and more forgiving than the more usual "creaming" method and creates a cake that is firm, but tender. The ganache-type frosting is rich, velvety and quick to prepare.

Black and White Layer Cake

SERVES 12 - 16

Dark Chocolate Frosting

1-1/4 cups Silk® soy creamer or non-dairy creamer

3-5 tablespoons sugar

1/4 stick (2 tablespoons) unsalted non-dairy margarine, room temperature

20 ounces non-dairy semisweet chocolate (see page 15, for brands), finely chopped

Golden Sour Creem Base Cake

2/3 cup Tofutti® Better Than Sour Cream

1/4 cup warm water

2-2/3 cups sifted cake flour, spooned into measuring cups

1 teaspoon baking powder

3/4 teaspoon baking soda

1/2 teaspoon salt

1-1/3 cups sugar

1-1/2 sticks (12 tablespoons) unsalted non-dairy margarine (such as Fleischmann's®), softened about 15 minutes until pliable and cut into tablespoon-sized pieces

2 large eggs, room temperature

2 large egg whites, room temperature

3/4 teaspoon vanilla extract

To get the cakes out of the pans, run a knife around the perimeter of the cakes to loosen the edges. Invert the pans onto cardboard cake boards, remove the parchment paper, top with another cake board and re-invert so the cakes are right-side-up.

1. For the frosting, heat about 1-1/2 inches of water in the bottom of a double boiler until hot, but not simmering. Place the creamer, sugar (the amount will vary with the brand of chocolate you are using and personal taste) and the margarine, in the top of the double boiler. Place it over the hot water, stirring until the sugar melts and the creamer is steaming. Add the chocolate to the creamer, stir and heat until the chocolate is completely melted. Strain the frosting into a bowl and set it aside to cool. If it's not thick enough to spread by the time the cake is ready to be assembled, refrigerate it briefly.

2. Preheat the oven to 350 degrees F. with a rack in the lower third of the oven. Grease two 9-inch round cake pans, line with kosher parchment paper (such as Reynolds®), grease the paper and then flour the pans.

3. In a medium bowl, whisk together the sour cream substitute and the water.

4. Into a large mixer bowl, sift together the flour, baking powder, baking soda and salt. Stir in the sugar.

5. Add the margarine and 3/4 of the Tofutti® mixture to the flour mixture. Beat on low until blended. Increase the speed to medium, and beat for 2 minutes until smooth and aerated.

Serve immediately or refrigerate in a covered cake holder for up to 3 days. Leave the cake at room temperature for 1 hour before serving.

The cake can be frozen for 3 months. Freeze it before wrapping so the frosting won't stick to the foil. To defrost, loosen the foil, or transfer the cake to a covered cake-holder. Defrost in the refrigerator, overnight. Let the cake stand at room temperature for 1 hour before serving.

6. Whisk the eggs, whites and vanilla into the remaining Tofutti mixture. Add to the batter a third at a time, beating on medium-low after each addition. Scrape down the bowl, and beat just to blend. Divide the mixture between the two pans. Tap the pans to remove bubbles. **Bake for 25-27 minutes** until a cake tester inserted into the center of the cakes come out clean. The cakes will not be very brown. Cool the cakes, in the pans, on a cooling rack. Remove the cakes from the pans (see sidebar, previous page).

7. To assemble the cake, leave one layer on a cake-board. Spread about 3/8-inch of frosting over the layer. Place the second layer on top. Spread frosting on the sides and then swirl the frosting over the top. If desired, you can pipe a border of frosting around the bottom perimeter of the cake.

Tiramisu

For me, tiramisu will never go out of style. I used to eat it out often, guzzling Lactaid® pills so that it wouldn't make me sick. Now, I can eat it with abandon! To have it dairy-free, is truly a dream come true. This variation is slightly cheesy, soft and light. It's flavored with coffee, creem, chocolate and a hint of Marsala. If you are short on time, packaged ladyfingers may be used in place of homemade ones. They don't usually contain dairy, but be sure to check.

Savoiardi (Ladyfingers))
3/4 cup sifted cake flour, spooned into a measuring cup
1/4 teaspoon salt

3 large eggs, room temperature and separated (be sure all tools and bowls are grease-free)
1/2 teaspoon vanilla extract
6 tablespoons sugar, divided

1/4 teaspoon cream of tartar
Powdered sugar in a sifter

Filling
2 tablespoons water
3 large pasteurized egg yolks, room temperature (*for regular eggs, directions follow)
1/2 cup sugar

8 ounces Tofutti Better Than Cream Cheese®, room temperature
1/2 stick (4 tablespoons) unsalted non-dairy margarine (such as Fleischmann's®), room temperature

3/4 cup Richwhip®, thawed

Tips

If you overbeat the egg whites so that they are stiff and dry, the cake will not rise properly. You'll know if you have over-beaten them because they'll ball up and look like little bits of Styrofoam when you try to fold them into your batter. If this happens, beat another egg white into the remaining egg whites and then continue to fold these into the batter.

If you have trouble visualizing size, draw the shapes on the curled side of the parchment. Turn the parchment over so that when you start piping, you will not be piping onto the ink.

If you don't want to pipe out the ladyfingers, spoon the batter onto the parchment paper, shaping it with two regular, oblong soup spoons. These will be fatter than the ones that are piped but will work just fine.

Soaking Syrup
3/4 cup hot brewed coffee
2 tablespoons sugar
2 tablespoons marsala wine, rum, Godiva®, or Kahlúa® liqueur (*for kosher, see page 28)

Topping
1 ounce finely grated non-dairy semisweet chocolate

1. Preheat the oven to 400 degrees F. with racks in the upper and lower thirds of the oven. Line 2 cookie sheets with kosher parchment paper (such as Reynolds®).

2. In a small bowl, mix together the flour and salt. Set aside. Place the egg yolks in a large mixer bowl. Beat on medium speed, adding 1/4 cup sugar gradually. When all of the sugar has been added, increase the speed to high and beat until the egg mixture forms a "ribbon" (see page 22). Beat in the vanilla. Sift the flour mixture into the egg yolks, but do not mix together.

3. Transfer the egg whites to a large, clean, grease-free mixer bowl. Add the cream of tartar and using clean, grease-free beaters, beat the egg whites until very foamy throughout. Gradually add the remaining sugar and then beat the whites just until they form soft peaks. Gently fold the eggs from the bottom of the bowl to

Tips

the top. Continue to beat the eggs until stiff, but not dry (see page 21). Stir 1/3 of the whites into the batter. Gently fold in the remaining egg whites.

4. Spoon the batter into a pastry bag with a 3/4-inch round tip. Pipe ladyfingers 3-1/2 x 1-inch wide, leaving 1/2 inch between each ladyfinger.

5. Sift powdered sugar over the ladyfingers. Let them rest a few seconds and then sprinkle on more powdered sugar. **Bake 4 minutes**. Move the top cookie sheet to the lower rack and the lower cookie sheet to the top rack. **Bake 4 - 6 minutes** more until the ladyfingers are golden. Remove the sheets from the oven and slide the parchment paper onto cooling racks. Remove the ladyfingers from the parchment paper before they cool completely. The ladyfingers can be made 2 days ahead of assembly or can be frozen for up to 3 months. Defrost them before using.

6. Before making the filling, preheat the oven broiler. Place the ladyfingers on a cookie sheet, flat side up and broil them about 6 inches from the heat source, until the flat sides look toasted and firm (1 - 2 minutes). Set aside to cool.

7. For the filling: Boil 2-inches water in the bottom of a double boiler.

8. In a metal mixer bowl (preferably with a handle) or in the top of the double boiler,

Tips

If using regular eggs, increase the water to 4 tablespoons. Whisk the water, 3 egg yolks and 1/2 cup sugar in a shallow metal bowl. Simmer 2-inches water in a skillet. Have a rubber scraper, instant-read thermometer, a timer and a large mixer bowl near the stove. Place the shallow bowl into the simmering water, and cook the egg mixture to 160 degrees F. (30 – 60 seconds), rapidly stirring with a rubber scraper and checking the temperature every 15 seconds. Transfer the mixture to a large mixer bowl and continue with the recipe.

whisk the water and egg yolks. Gradually whisk in the sugar.

9. Set the bowl over the boiling water and whisk until the eggs reach 120 - 130 degrees F. (very warm, but not so hot that they hurt your finger). It will take only a minute or two. Remove the bowl from the heat and beat the mixture until it is room temperature and the egg mixture is pale and thick (about 5 - 8 minutes).

10. Place the cream cheese substitute and the margarine into a large bowl and blend the two together with a wooden spoon (DO NOT BEAT or the mixture will get watery).

11. Stir 1 cup of the egg mixture into the Tofutti mixture. Gently, whisk until smooth. Fold in the remainder of the eggs.

12. In a small bowl, beat the Richwhip® on high speed until it forms moderately firm peaks. Fold into the egg mixture.

13. For the syrup, combine the hot coffee, sugar and marsala in a small bowl. Stir until the sugar dissolves.

14. To assemble the tiramisu, dip half of the ladyfingers into the warm syrup, and place, flat side up, in an 8 x 8-inch square glass baking dish. The whole bottom of the pan should be covered. Spoon on half of the filling. Dip the remaining ladyfingers and place flat side down into the

filling. Spoon on the remaining filling. Cover the pan with nonstick foil and refrigerate overnight. Before serving, sprinkle the top with grated chocolate. Cut the Tiramisu into portions and use a small, square spatula to remove them from the pan (the first piece may be difficult to remove).

VARIATIONS
Individual tiramisu can be made in champagne glasses. Make several layers as directed above, but add grated chocolate on top of each layer of filling to delineate the layers.

This rolled cake is an absolute show-stopper. The buttercreem is creamy, rich and full-flavored and nuts provide just the right amount of crunch. For a cake roll, you need a spongy sheet cake that will be very flexible so you don't have to worry about tearing it as you roll it. One trick to making sure that it rolls nicely is to roll it up in a towel while the cake is still hot. When it cools, it's unrolled, filled and re-rolled without any trouble.

Maple Walnut Roulade

SERVES 8

Sponge Sheet Base Cake
2/3 cup sifted cake flour, spooned into measuring cups
Pinch salt
2 large eggs, room temperature
3 large eggs, room temperature, separated (be sure all tools and bowls are grease-free)
1/3 cup plus 1 tablespoon sugar, divided
1/2 teaspoon vanilla extract
1/8 teaspoon cream of tartar
Powdered sugar

Hazelnut Simple Syrup
3 tablespoons water
3 tablespoons sugar
1 tablespoon hazelnut or other liqueur (for kosher, see page 28)

Maple Buttercreem
2 sticks (16 tablespoons) unsalted non-dairy margarine (such as Fleischmann's®), cold and cut into tablespoon-size chunks
2 tablespoons water
4 large pasteurized egg yolks (for regular eggs, directions follow)

If you overbeat the egg whites so that they are stiff and dry, the cake will not rise properly. You'll know if you have over-beaten them because they'll ball up and look like little bits of Styrofoam when you try to fold them into your batter. If this happens, add another egg white into the beaten egg whites, and beat briefly to combine. Continue to fold the egg whites into the batter using all but 1/2 cup of them (to account for the extra egg white that you added).

2/3 cup sugar

1/3 cup pure maple syrup

1/4 teaspoon pure vanilla extract

1/2 teaspoon pure maple extract

2 cups shelled walnuts, chopped medium-fine

1. Preheat the oven to 400 degrees F. Cut a piece of kosher parchment paper (such as Reynolds®) to fit a 13 x 18-inch jelly-roll pan. Remove the parchment from the pan and then grease and flour it. Spray a few dots of grease into the bottom of the pan (to hold down the parchment) and then return the parchment paper to the pan (for maximum volume, the sides of sponge cake pans should not be greased).

2. In a small bowl, sift the flour with the salt.

3. Place the 2 whole eggs and the egg yolks into a mixer bowl. Beat on medium-high, adding 1/3 cup sugar as you beat. Continue to beat for 5 - 7 minutes, until the mixture is light in texture and color, and forms a "ribbon" (a spoonful of batter dropped from a spoon should fall in a ribbon and remain on the surface of the eggs for a second or two before disappearing). Beat in the vanilla.

4. Sift the flour-salt mixture over the egg mixture, but do not mix in.

5. Place the egg whites in a clean, dry and grease-free bowl. Using grease-free beaters, beat the egg whites with the cream

Tips

The spongecake base can be made a day in adnvance and stored in a plastic bag at room temperature (leave it rolled up). It can also be frozen for up to 3 months. Defrost, at room temperature, overnight.

of tartar until very foamy throughout. Continue beating, adding the remaining 1 tablespoon of sugar until it forms peaks that are stiff but not dry (see sidebar, previous page). Stir 1/3 of the whites into the egg yolk mixture. Gently fold in the remaining whites. Turn the mixture into the prepared pan and gently spread it evenly to the edges of the pan (an offset spatula works best). **Bake for 7 - 10 minutes** until the cake is golden and springy.

6. Using a small, sharp knife and an up-and-down sawing motion, cut the edges of the cake away from the sides of the pan.

7. Sprinkle some powdered sugar onto a clean, cotton, dish towel. Turn the pan upside down onto the towel so that there is an excess of 3 inches of towel at one short end of the cake. Remove the pan and the parchment paper from the bottom of the cake. Fold the excess towel over the short side of the cake and then roll the cake up in the towel. Let it cool completely.

8. For the simple syrup, combine all ingredients in a small pot. Heat over medium heat until the sugar dissolves and then raise the heat and bring to a boil. Stir in the liqueur (if you want the flavor, but not the alcohol, add the liqueur before bringing the mixture to a boil). Let cool before using. The soaking syrup can be made up to 3 weeks ahead (keep in the refrigerator, but bring to room temperature before using).

If using regular eggs, increase the water to 4 tablespoons. In a shallow metal bowl, whisk together the water, 4 eggs, 2/3 cup sugar and the maple syrup. Simmer 1-inch of water in a skillet. Have a rubber scraper, instant-read thermometer, a timer and a large mixer bowl near the stove. Place the shallow bowl into the simmering water, and cook the egg mixture to 160 degrees F. (30 – 60 seconds), rapidly stirring with a rubber scraper and checking the temperature every 15 seconds. Transfer the mixture to a large mixer bowl and continue with the recipe.

The cake may be stored in the refrigerator for up to 3 days. Let it stand at room temperature 1 hour, before serving, to allow the buttercream to soften.

Freeze the filled roulade before wrapping it in foil. To defrost, loosen the foil, or transfer the cake to a covered cake-holder. Defrost in the refrigerator, overnight. Let the cake stand at room temperature for 1 hour before serving.

9. To make the frosting, place the cold margarine in a large mixer bowl. Set it aside while you prepare the rest of the frosting.

10. Bring 2 inches of water to boil in the bottom of a double boiler. In a large, metal mixer bowl that fits the double boiler, whisk together the water, egg yolks, sugar and maple syrup. Set the bowl over the simmering water, and whisk constantly for 1 - 3 minutes, until the mixture is about 120 degrees F. (warm, but not hot enough to feel uncomfortable to your finger).

11. Remove the mixer bowl from the heat and beat on medium-high speed for 10 - 15 minutes, until the mixture is room temperature.

12. In a large mixer bowl, beat the margarine for a few minutes, until it's creamy, scraping the bowl down periodically. On medium-low, beat in the egg yolk mixture in three additions. When all of the egg yolk has been added, increase the speed and beat the frosting until it forms an emulsion and looks like frosting (about 10 minutes). Beat in the vanilla and maple extract.

13. To assemble, unroll the cake. Dab on the soaking syrup. Using about 2/3 of the frosting, spread a thin layer over the cake. Sprinkle half of the walnuts over the frosting. Roll the cake up from the frosted short end. Spread a thin layer of frosting on the outside of the cake. Finely chop the remaining walnuts and sprinkle them over the cake.

Frosted Cupcakes

SERVES 12

Those of you who have children with allergies or lactose intolerance, will find these easy cupcakes a God-send; great to send to school and for birthdays. To get a kid's perspective, the frosting was taste-tested by Samantha and Bradley Del Vecchio. When offered a choice between this fluffy, lightly sweetened frosting and a typical bakery-style powdered sugar frosting, both children preferred this.

However, I'm a huge advocate of choice, hence Simple Vanilla Frosting follows!

Cupcakes
1-1/2 cups sifted cake flour
3/4 cup all-purpose flour, fluffed, scooped and leveled into a measuring cup
1-1/2 teaspoons baking powder
1 teaspoon baking soda
1/4 teaspoon salt
1-1/8 cups sugar

1-1/2 sticks (12 tablespoons) unsalted nondairy margarine (such as Fleischmann's®) cold
1-1/8 cups Tofutti® Better Than Sour Cream, room temperature
1-1/2 teaspoons vanilla extract
3 large eggs, room temperature

Simple Vanilla Buttercreem
1 pound jar Marshmallow Fluff®
2-1/2 sticks (20 tablespoons) unsalted nondairy margarine, softened 15 minutes at room temperature, divided
1 teaspoon vanilla extract
1-2 tablespoons corn syrup, to taste

Food coloring
Sprinkles

Unfrosted cupcakes can be frozen on a baking sheet and then transferred to a plastic bag. They may be defrosted at room temperature, or on microwave-defrost for 15 seconds, or until thawed.

1. Preheat the oven to 350 degrees F. with a rack in the middle of the oven. Grease and flour a muffin pan with 12 cups.

2. In a large mixer bowl, sift together both flours, baking powder, baking soda and salt. Stir in the sugar. Add the margarine, 3/4 of the Tofutti and the vanilla. Beat on low, until blended. Increase the speed to medium and beat for 2 minutes, until smooth and aerated.

3. In a small bowl, whisk together the eggs and the remaining Tofutti. Add this to the batter in three additions, beating on medium-low after each addition. Scrape down the bowl and beat until blended.

4. Spoon the batter into the muffin pan, filling each cup 1/2 – 3/4 full, depending on how big you'd like the muffins to be. Rap the pans on the counter to remove any air pockets. **Bake for 15 - 20 minutes** until the muffins are golden brown and a tester inserted into the muffins comes out with no moist crumbs attached. Set the muffin pan on a cooling rack for 5 minutes. Run a skewer around the perimeter of each muffin, and then turn them out of pan. Set them right-side-up, and let cool completely.

5. For the frosting, beat the margarine, in a large mixer bowl, until creamy. Beat in the Fluff, in 2 additions. Beat in the vanilla. Continue to beat, on medium-high,

The frosted cupcakes will keep for a few days, in the refrigerator, in a covered container. Leave at room temperature for 10 minutes before serving.

To freeze frosted cupcakes, freeze them in one layer, in a covered container. Defrost them, in the refrigerator, overnight.

for 2 minutes or until the frosting is fluffy and light and no longer marshmallowy. If not sweet enough, beat in corn syrup to taste.

6.   Divide the frosting into different bowls and add food coloring, if desired. If you'd like to have some frosting inside of each cupcake, place some of the frosting in a pastry bag with a Bismarck tip, and pipe in frosting until it starts coming out the top. Spread frosting over the cupcakes and top with sprinkles. If you prefer the icing to be a little firmer, refrigerate the cupcakes for 15 minutes before serving.

VARIATIONS

Sour Creem Birthday Cake – The batter can be made in two 9-inch round cake pans. Grease, line with parchment and flour the pans. Bake for 25-30 minutes until a tester comes out clean. For a layer cake, double the frosting recipe. It can also be made in a 9 x 12-inch pan. Bake for 30-40 minutes.

Simple Vanilla Frosting

MAKES ENOUGH FOR 12 CUPCAKES OR ONE 8-INCH CAKE

Simple Vanilla Frosting
2 sticks (16 tablespoons) unsalted nondairy margarine (such as Fleischmann's), softened
4 cups 10x powdered sugar, sifted and divided
2 tablespoons dairy-case soymilk (such as Silk®)
1 teaspoon vanilla or other flavoring

In a large mixer bowl, beat the margarine until creamy. Beat in 3-3/4 cups powdered sugar, 1 cup at a time, until smooth. If using the frosting for decorating, beat in the milk and vanilla until smooth and lightened in texture. Frost the cakes. If using the frosting for decorating, beat in the remaining 1/4 cup powdered sugar, if using the frosting for decorating. Keep covered until ready to use.

I never serve Simple Vanilla Frosting because it's much too sweet for most adults and my kids prefer buttercream. However, if yours like it sweet, this one's for them.

PASTRY

This simple and simply scrumptious crisp is easy to assemble and ready to eat within an hour. Because it bakes at high temperature for only a brief time, the texture and flavor of the berries is preserved. Bake it in a large pan for a homey dessert or in individual ramekins for elegant presentation. It tastes great with a scoop of vanilla ice creem melting on the top.

Blueberry Crisp

SERVES 4 - 6

Crumb Topping (Streusel)
3/4 cup all-purpose flour, fluffed, scooped and leveled into measuring cups
1/4 cup sifted cake flour, spooned into a measuring cup
1/4 cup packed light brown sugar
1/4 cup granulated sugar
1/4 teaspoon cinnamon
5 tablespoons unsalted non-dairy stick margarine (such as Fleischmann's®), melted

4 cups fresh blueberries, washed
6 tablespoons sugar
1/2 teaspoon cinnamon
2 tablespoons cornstarch

1 tablespoon orange juice
1/2 cup boiling water

1. Preheat the oven to 400 degrees F. with a rack in the middle of the oven.

2. For the crumb topping, mix the flours, sugars, cinnamon and margarine in a small bowl. Pinch the mixture to form clumps.

3. Place the berries in a 2-quart casserole or in a large bowl, if you plan to use ra-

Blueberry Crisp can be made a few days ahead. Cover it, and store in the refrigerator. Reheat in a 350 degree F. oven until just warm, about 5 - 15 minutes, depending on the size of the dish and the depth of the berries.

mekins. Stir in the sugar, cinnamon and cornstarch. Add the orange juice and boiling water.

4. For individual portions, spoon the fruit mixture into 3/4 – 1 cup ramekins (custard cups). Set the ramekins on a baking pan to catch drips.

5. Sprinkle the crumb topping over the blueberry mixture. **Bake for 20 - 25 minutes** until the crumbs are nicely browned and firm, and the berry mixture looks juicy.

6. Remove the crisp(s) from the oven and cool for 30 - 45 minutes until just warm. Blueberry Crisp tastes great with a scoop of Vanilla Ice Creem (page 36) on top.

VARIATIONS
Blueberry Crumb Pie – Use a fully baked 8 or 9-inch pie shell. (For example Sweet Pastry Crust, page 173, baked an extra **5 - 10 minutes**, until well browned.) Fill with the berry mixture. Top with the crumbs and **bake 20 – 25 minutes**.

To create a flaky crust, I use shortening and add margarine and sugar for flavor. Using some cake flour ensures that the crust will be tender. Doughs made with margarine are softer than those made with butter, so I recommend refrigerating the dough overnight. For the filling, I like Granny Smith apples for their texture, Golden Delicious for sweetness, and McIntosh for tart apple flavor. Use spices to suit your taste.

Apple Pie

SERVES 6 - 8
MAKE DOUGH 1 DAY AHEAD

Flaky Pie Crust
2 cups all-purpose flour, fluffed, scooped and leveled into measuring cups
1/2 cup sifted cake flour, spooned into a measuring cup
1 teaspoon salt
1 tablespoon sugar
10 tablespoons shortening, frozen and cut into 1/2-inch cubes
1/2 stick plus 1 tablespoon (5 tablespoons total) unsalted non-dairy stick margarine (such as Fleischmann's®), frozen and cut into 1/4-inch slices
1/4 cup ice water, divided

Filling
5 medium Granny Smith apples
1 medium golden Delicious apple
2 medium McIntosh apples
1 cup packed light brown sugar
1 teaspoon cinnamon
1/8 teaspoon nutmeg
1/4 cup cornstarch
1 tablespoon unsalted non-dairy stick margarine, cut into 1/4-inch cubes

Glaze
1 large egg white, whisked
1 teaspoon sugar

Tips

For a foolproof rolling method, cut open a jumbo zip-top bag so that it is hinged on one long side. Flour the inside of the plastic and place the dough inside. Roll the dough to 1/8-inch thickness, flipping the plastic over and flouring the dough as necessary.

1. Place the flours, salt and sugar in a food processor bowl. Pulse to mix everything together. Place the shortening and margarine on top of the dry ingredients. Pulse until the fats are cut into pea-size bits. Transfer the mixture to a bowl. Sprinkle on 3 tablespoons ice water. Mix with a fork and then, using your fingertips, press the mixture into a solid mass. If necessary, add more water to bring the dough together. Divide the dough in half. Wrap each piece in plastic wrap and refrigerate overnight.

2. Preheat the oven to 425 degrees F. with a rack in the middle of the oven. Grease and flour an 8-inch glass pie plate.

3. Roll 1 piece of dough into an 11 or 12-inch circle about 1/8-inch thick (see sidebar). Fold the dough into quarters, transfer the dough to the pie plate and open the dough up so that it fits into the pan. There should be several inches of overhang. Trim the dough to 1/4-inch beyond the rim.

4. For the filling, peel, core and cut the apples into 1/4-inch slices. Place 10 cups apples into a large bowl along with the brown sugar, cinnamon, nutmeg and cornstarch. Discard any remaining apples.

5. Roll out the remaining dough making it larger than the bottom crust, so that it will fit over the mounded apples. Spoon the fruit into the crust-lined pie plate,

For best results, the pie should not be made more than 8 hours in advance (leave uncovered at room temperature). Rewarm it at 350 degrees F. for 15 minutes. Leftover pie should be covered and refrigerated. Heat at 350 degrees F. to re-crisp the top crust.

mounding it high in the pan. Dot with the margarine. Add the top crust. Trim the top crust so it is the same size as the bottom crust. Squeeze the two edges together and then roll the edge up to make a nice border on the pan rim. Flute the edge with your thumbs or use a fork to press the edge down (see drawing of fluting, page 175). Make 4 or 5 slits in the pie with a sharp knife. Brush the crust with the whisked egg white and sprinkle with the sugar.

6. Place the pie on a baking sheet. **Bake the pie for 25 minutes**. Reduce the temperature to 375 degrees F. and **bake for another 30 - 40 minutes** more until both the top and bottom crusts are golden. Cool at least 30 minutes before eating.

Pecan Pie

Most pecan pie is layered, with a gelatinous bottom and a nut-studded top. It usually contains butter, but you'll note that there is no butter substitute in this filling. Deleting the butter and adding extra nuts creates a uniform filling of gooey caramel, with nuts spread throughout. The crust contains egg yolk, which keeps it crisp even upon refrigeration.

Sweet Pastry Crust

1-1/2 cups all-purpose flour, fluffed, scooped and leveled into measuring cups

2 tablespoons sugar

1/4 teaspoon salt

1 stick (8 tablespoons) unsalted non-dairy margarine (such as Fleischmann's®), frozen and cut into 1/4-inch slices

1 large egg yolk

1 - 3 teaspoons water

Filling

3 large eggs

1 cup sugar

1 cup dark corn syrup

1 teaspoon vanilla extract

2 cups chopped pecans

Garnish (optional)

16 pecan halves

Dark corn syrup

1 eight-ounce carton Richwhip®, thawed and whipped or Vanilla Ice Creem, page 36

Flouring the plate is controversial, as there is a risk that the dough could shrink off of the pie plate rim. Pie weights help prevent this, and it is much easier to get slices out of the pan when the plate is floured.

Cut out a shield for the pie edges from a piece of aluminum foil if you do not have a molded shield.

1. Place the flour, sugar and salt in a food processor bowl. Pulse until the ingredients are well mixed.

2. Add the frozen margarine. Pulse about 7 times, until the margarine is cut into lentil-sized pieces. Turn the processor on and add the egg yolk and 1 teaspoon water, through the feed tube. Process for 10 seconds. If not yet clumping, add another teaspoon of water. Process 10 seconds more. If necessary, add the remaining water, and process again. The dough should be dry, but should be able to be pinched together. Dump the dough out onto a board and press into a flattened disk. Wrap in plastic wrap and refrigerate 15 minutes.

3. Preheat the oven to 375 degrees F. Grease and flour a 9-inch glass pie plate.

4. Cut open a jumbo zip-top bag so that it is hinged on one long side. Flour the inside of the plastic and add the dough. Roll the dough into a 12-inch round, about 1/16-inch thick, flipping the plastic over and flouring the dough as necessary.

5. This dough is too tender to be folded for transfer to the pie plate. Place your palm under the plastic and then upturn the plastic onto the pie plate. The dough is very supple, so that cracks and breaks can be fixed by simply pinching it back together.

6. Cut the dough so that it extends 1/4 inch beyond the pie plate rim and then roll it up so that it rests on the rim (see diagrams next page). Use your thumbs to flute the

Cut the dough so that it extends
1/4-inch past the rim.

Then roll the dough up
onto the rim.

Fluting the pie crust.

Serve the pie either cold or at room temperature. It will be softer at room temperature, and stickier and more gooey if cold. Serve with whipped Richwhip® or ice creem, if desired.

edge, or use the tines of a fork to make the border (see sidebar). Press a piece of nonstick aluminum foil into the crust, nonstick side touching the dough and fill the foil with dried beans or pie weights.

7. **Bake for 10 minutes**. Remove the foil and beans. **Bake for 5 - 10 minutes** more until the dough is partially baked and just barely starting to brown. Cool on a wire rack.

8. Increase the oven temperature to 425 degrees F.

9. In a large bowl, lightly whisk the eggs. Whisk in the sugar. Stir in the corn syrup, vanilla and nuts. Pour into the partially baked pie shell.

10. **Bake for 5 minutes**. Lower the oven temperature to 325 degrees F. Open the oven door for 5 minutes to reduce heat. Shield the crust edges with an aluminum shield. **Bake for 30 minutes** more. Cover the top with foil if it's browning too much. **Bake for another 25 - 35 minutes**, until set. (Total baking time is about 60 - 65 minutes). The filling should not shake when you move it. Transfer the pie to a wire rack.

11. To garnish, brush the whole pecans with a little corn syrup and stick them to the pie, placed around the perimeter, like the markings on a clock-face. Let the pie cool completely. Wrap it with foil or plastic wrap and refrigerate overnight.

This traditional pie is creamy yet firm. For the best flavor and texture, use canned pumpkin and non-dairy creamer instead of soy creamer. The Sweeter Pastry Crust is used because it doesn't get soggy in the refrigerator and it tastes great with the pumpkin. For maximum flavor, serve the pie 1 - 2 days after making it, garnished with whipped Richwhip®.

Pumpkin Pie

SERVES 8 - 10
MAKE DOUGH 2 DAYS AHEAD

Sweeter Pastry Crust

1-1/2 cups all-purpose flour, fluffed, scooped and leveled into measuring cups
4 tablespoons granulated sugar
1/4 teaspoon salt

1 stick (8 tablespoons) unsalted non-dairy margarine (such as Fleischmann's®), frozen and cut into 1/4-inch slices
1 large egg yolk
1 – 3 teaspoons water

Filling

2 large eggs
14-ounce can pumpkin
1 cup packed light brown sugar
1/2 teaspoon ground ginger
1/4 teaspoon cloves
1 teaspoon cinnamon
1 tablespoon all-purpose flour
1/2 teaspoon salt
1 cup non-dairy creamer (not soy)

Garnish (optional)

1 eight-ounce container of Richwhip®, thawed and whipped

Tips

Flouring the plate is controversial, as there is a risk that the dough could shrink off of the pie plate rim. Pie weights help prevent this, and it is much easier to get the slices out of the pan when the plate is floured. However, it's so much easier to get the slices out of the pan when the plate is floured, that I do it anyway. Using pie weights will prevent bubbles, and will help keep the dough from shrinking too much. Cut out a shield for the pie edges from a piece of aluminum foil if you do not have a molded shield.

1. Place the flour, sugar and salt in a food processor bowl. Pulse until the ingredients are well mixed.

2. Add the frozen margarine. Pulse about 7 times, until the margarine is cut into lentil-sized pieces. Turn the processor on and add the egg yolk and 1 teaspoon water, through the feed tube. Process for 10 seconds. If not yet clumping, add another teaspoon of water. Process 10 seconds more. If necessary, add the remaining water, and process again. The dough should be dry, but should be able to be pinched together. Dump the dough out onto a board and press into a flattened disk. Wrap in plastic wrap and refrigerate 15 minutes.

3. Preheat the oven to 375 degrees F. Grease and flour a 9-inch glass pie plate.

4. Cut open a jumbo zip-top bag so that it is hinged on one long side. Flour the inside of the plastic and add the dough. Roll the dough into a 12-inch round, about 1/16-inch thick, flipping the plastic over and flouring the dough as necessary.

5. This dough is too tender to be folded for transfer to the pie plate. Place your palm under the plastic and then upturn the plastic onto the pie plate. The dough is very supple, so that cracks and breaks can be fixed by simply pinching it back together. Cut the dough so that it extends 1/4 inch

Pumpkin pie tastes best if made 1 - 2 days before serving. It will keep in the refrigerator for another 2 - 3 days.

beyond the pie plate rim and then roll it up so that it rests on the rim. Use your thumbs to flute the edge, or use the tines of a fork to make the border (see drawing, page 175). Press a piece of nonstick aluminum foil into the crust, nonstick side touching the dough, and fill the foil with dried beans or pie weights.

6. **Bake for 10 minutes.** Remove the foil and beans. **Bake for 5 - 10 minutes** more until the dough is just barely starting to brown. Cool on a wire rack.

7. Preheat the oven to 425 degrees F. with a rack in the middle of the oven. Make a pie crust edge shield out of aluminum foil if you don't have a molded edge shield.

8. In a large mixer bowl, lightly whisk the eggs. Stir (do not beat) in the pumpkin, brown sugar, spices, flour and salt. Stir in the creamer. Pour the filling into the pie crust and **bake 15 minutes**. Reduce the heat to 350 degrees F. Place a shield on the edges of the crust and continue to **bake for 50 minutes** more until the pumpkin is set and firm.

9. Cool completely on a wire rack. Cover the pie with plastic wrap and refrigerate overnight. Before serving, gently mop up any liquid that has accumulated on the top of the pie. Serve the pie, cold, garnished with whipped Richwhip®.

I love this oil-based press-in crumb-style crust because it's so easy to make and uses ingredients that I always have on hand. It's filled with a typical French almond filling (frangipane) and topped with fresh, seasonal berries. For a great presentation, place strawberry slices around the perimeter of the tart with mounds of berries in the center. See the photo at the beginning of the book for a look at this extraordinary dessert.

Berry Frangipane Tart

SERVES 8 - 10

Toasted Almond Crumb Crust
1 tablespoon unsalted non-dairy margarine (such as Fleischmann's®), softened
1-1/2 cups sliced almonds, divided
1-1/2 cups all-purpose flour, fluffed, scooped and leveled into measuring cups
1/4 cup sugar
1/2 cup canola oil

Toasted Almond Frangipane Filling
1 cup toasted almonds, reserved from above
1/3 cup sugar
1 tablespoon all-purpose flour
7/8 stick (7 tablespoons) unsalted non-dairy margarine, softened
1 large egg, room temperature
1 tablespoon amaretto liqueur (Amaretto di Saronno®, for kosher)

3-5 cups berries of choice
1/2 cup seedless jelly or jam

1. Preheat the oven to 350 degrees F. With 1 tablespoon of margarine, generously grease a 9-inch tart pan with removable bottom.

2. Place the almonds in a baking pan and set in the oven for 3 - 5 minutes until the

The baked crust can be made up to 8 hours ahead. Leave it at room temperature, uncovered, until ready to use. The tart with the filling can be made 8 hours ahead, if refrigeratred.

Once the berries have been placed on the tart, it should be refrigerated for at least 1 hour to allow the jam and juices to seep into the filling, but should be served within 4 hours.

Serve the tart cold or at room temperature.

almonds are fragrant and just barely starting to brown. Set aside. Increase the oven temperature to 425 degrees F. Reserve 1 cup of nuts to be used in the filling.

3. Place the remaining 1/2 cup of nuts in a food processor along with the flour and sugar. Pulse on and off until the nuts are finely ground. With the processor running, pour the oil through the feed tube and process until the mixture starts to clump up. Pack the mixture into the sides of the prepared 9-inch tart pan so that they are a scant 1/8-inch thick. Press the remainder into the bottom of the pan. **Bake for 12 - 15 minutes** until the tart is lightly browned. Set aside to cool. Reduce the oven temperature to 375 degrees F.

4. For the filling place the reserved cup of almonds, the sugar and flour in the processor bowl. Pulse until the nuts are finely chopped. Add the margarine and pulse until blended. Add the egg and the liqueur and process until all is blended. Pour the mixture into the baked crust. **Bake for 15 - 25 minutes** or until firm and lightly browned. Let cool.

5. Brush some of the jam over the filling. If using strawberries, wash, dry, hull and slice them lengthwise into scant 1/8-inch slices. If using blueberries, raspberries or blackberries, wash them and pat dry. The berries can be mixed with the jelly or glazed with it. Raspberries, especially, taste better when they are brushed rather than saturated with the jelly. Arrange or pile on the berries using more if piled, and fewer berries if they are arranged.

Banana Toffee Tart

SERVES 8 - 10

There are lots of steps to this recipe, but the results are well worth the effort. If you make the tart in stages over a couple of days, it will seem effortless, and what could be better than the combination of toffee, bananas and pecans!

Toffee Topping

2/3 cup packed light brown sugar

1/4 stick (2 tablespoons) unsalted non-dairy margarine (such as Fleischmann's®), room temperature

1/4 cup Silk® soy creamer or non-dairy creamer

1/4 teaspoon vanilla extract

Pecan Crust

1 tablespoon unsalted non-dairy stick margarine, softened

1-1/2 cups pecan pieces, divided

1-1/2 cups all-purpose flour, fluffed, scooped and leveled into measuring cups

4 tablespoons granulated sugar

8 tablespoons canola oil

Pecan Frangipane Filling

1 cup toasted pecan pieces, reserved from above

1/3 cup granulated sugar

1 tablespoon all-purpose flour

5/8 stick (5 tablespoons) unsalted non-dairy margarine, softened

1 large egg, room temperature

1 tablespoon rum

2 large bananas, ripe but firm

Garnish (optional)

Richwhip®, thawed and whipped, or ice creem

<u>*Toffee Topping*</u>
up to 3 days ahead – refrigerated

<u>*Crust*</u>
up to 8 hours ahead

<u>*Filled tart*</u>
up to 8 hours ahead – refrigerated

<u>*Topping and completed tart*</u>
up to 1 hour ahead

1. For the topping, combine the brown sugar, margarine and creamer in a medium saucepan. Heat over medium heat, stirring constantly, until the mixture starts to simmer. Stop stirring and simmer for 3 minutes. Stir in the vanilla. If not using immediately, pour the toffee into a container. Let it cool until warm, cover and refrigerate until ready to use.

2. For the crust, preheat the oven to 350 degrees F. With 1 tablespoon of margarine, generously grease a 9-inch tart pan with removable bottom. Place the pecans on a baking sheet lined with foil. Bake the pecans for 3 - 5 minutes until the pecans are fragrant and just barely starting to brown. Set aside 1 cup of nuts to be used in the filling. Increase the oven temperature to 425 degrees F.

3. Place the remaining 1/2 cup of pecans in a food processor along with the flour and sugar. Pulse until the nuts are finely ground. With the processor running, pour the oil through the feed tube and process until the mixture starts to clump up. Pack the mixture onto the sides of the prepared 9-inch tart pan so that they are a scant 1/8-inch thick, and then press the remainder into the bottom of the pan. **Bake for 12 - 15 minutes** until the tart is lightly browned. Cool. Reduce the oven temperature to 375 degrees F.

Once assembled, the tart can be left at room temperature or refrigerated for 1 - 2 hours before serving.

Serve with ice creem or whipped Richwhip®.

4. For the filling, place the reserved cup of toasted pecans, 1/3 cup sugar and 1 table-spoon flour into the food processor bowl. Pulse until the nuts are finely chopped. Add the margarine and pulse until blend-ed. Add the egg and the rum. Process until blended. Pour the mixture into the baked crust. **Bake for 15 minutes** or until set and lightly browned. Cool the tart on a wire rack. The tart shell can be refriger-ated for up to 8 hours.

5. Up to one hour before serving, slice the bananas into 1/8-inch rounds. Place the bananas on the tart in concentric circles. Reheat the toffee until just warm and slightly runny (15 - 30 seconds in a micro-wave). Brush the bananas with some of the toffee and then pour the remainder of the toffee evenly onto the tart. As soon as the toffee cools and firms up a bit, the tart is ready to be served (15 minutes or so).

This is a great tart to make at the last minute, because the dough does not have to be refrigerated before shaping it to fit the pan. The filling is a variation of a frangipane, flavored with hazelnuts and more custardy than the Berry Frangipane Tart (page 179). It's best served during the summer when peaches are at their height of perfection.

Peach Raspberry Tart

SERVES 8 - 10

Sweet Pastry Crust Sablé
1-1/4 cups all-purpose flour, fluffed, scooped and leveled into measuring cups
1/2 cup powdered sugar
1/8 teaspoon salt
1 stick (8 tablespoons) unsalted non-dairy margarine (such as Fleischmann's®), frozen
1 large egg yolk, cold
1 teaspoon cold water

Hazelnut Filling
1 cup skinned hazelnuts or macadamias
1/2 cup sugar
1 stick (8 tablespoons) unsalted non-dairy margarine, cool room temperature
2 large eggs, room temperature
1/4 cup all-purpose flour, fluffed, scooped and leveled into a measuring cup
3 tablespoons Frangelica® or amaretto liqueur (for kosher, see page 28)

Topping
1/2 cup seedless raspberry jam
1/2 cup apricot jam
1/2 teaspoon gelatin
   (directions for kosher gelatin follow)
1 tablespoon water
3 large, very ripe peaches, peeled
   (directions follow)

Skinned hazelnuts can be bought at www.kingarthurflour.com. To skin them yourself, place the hazelnuts on a pan, in a 350-degree oven. Roast for 10 minutes. Pour the nuts onto the upper half of a kitchen towel. Fold the bottom half of the towel up over the nuts and rub it back and forth over the nuts. The skins should come off.

1 medium lemon

Garnish
1 pint fresh raspberries

1. Preheat the oven to 375 degrees F. Grease an 8-inch tart pan with removable bottom.

2. For the crust: Mix the flour, sugar and salt in a food processor. Pulse to mix the ingredients together. Cut the margarine into 1/4-inch cubes and add to the processor. Pulse on and off, until the mixture looks like coarse meal. In a small bowl, whisk together the egg yolk and water. Add to the processor and process for 10 - 20 seconds, until the dough starts to come together. Turn the dough out onto a piece of plastic wrap and press it into a ball.

3. To fit the dough into the pan, start with gumball-sized lumps of dough. Squeeze the dough between your fingers until it is a scant 1/8-inch thick. Place in the pan. Repeat with the remaining dough, piecing everything together to make a solid crust. To trim the edges, run a rolling pin over the top of the pan. Press the edges up slightly to thin them out and to make the edges a little higher than the pan. Prick the bottom of the dough in several places with a fork. Freeze the tart for 15 minutes or until firm to the touch. Press nonstick aluminum foil snugly on top of

To peel peaches, fill a medium saucepan with water and bring it to a boil. Place the peaches in the boiling water for 30 - 60 seconds. Transfer the peaches to a bowl of ice water. Remove the peach skins with a sharp knife.

the dough with the nonstick side down. Fill the foil with pie weights or beans. **Bake for 15 minutes**, remove the foil and beans and **bake 10 – 15 minutes** more until lightly browned. Cool completely on a wire rack.

4. For the filling, process the nuts and sugar in a large food processor until finely ground Add the margarine and process until well blended and fluffy (about 10 - 20 seconds). With the processor running, add the eggs through the feed tube, processing until the mixture is smooth, about 30 seconds. Add the liqueur and process until well blended. Scrape the filling into the pie shell. Bake for 20 minutes, shielding the edges if they are getting too brown. Cool the tart completely on a wire rack.

5. Up to 8 hours before serving, place the raspberry jam in a microwave-safe bowl. Heat for 20 seconds or until the jam is melted and warm. Brush the raspberry jam over the tart.

6. Place the gelatin and 1 tablespoon water in a small bowl. Set it aside to soften. Strain the apricot preserves through a medium-mesh strainer into a small bowl. You should have 1/4 cup of lump-free apricot preserves.

7. Peel the peaches (directions in sidebar). Cut the peaches in half, remove the pits, and slice the peaches into 1/8-inch slices.

*For a kosher glaze, use Diet Kojel®
unflavored gelée. Heat the strained
apricot preserves with two teaspoons
of water, until simmering. Stir in the
gelée and brush onto the peaches
immediately.*

Squeeze the lemon into a bowl of ice water, slide in the peaches and then drain and pat dry. Set the peaches on the tart in concentric circles.

8. Heat the gelatin mixture in the microwave oven for 10 - 20 seconds until it liquefies. Stir the gelatin into the strained apricot preserves. Brush the apricot glaze generously over the peaches. Refrigerate until the glaze is set, up to 4 hours before serving. The raspberries can be scattered on the tart or served as a garnish on each plate.

Chocolate Creem Tart

SERVES 10 - 12
MAKE PASTRY AND DEFROST RICHWHIP 1 DAY AHEAD

This velvety and rich chocolate mousse tart is a slice of heaven and so easy to make! The crunchy and sandy texture of the sablé crust is perfect with the smooth, chocolate filling.

Sweet Pastry Crust Sablé
1-1/4 cups all-purpose flour, fluffed, scooped and leveled into measuring cups
1/2 cup powdered sugar
1/8 teaspoon salt
1 stick (8 tablespoons) unsalted non-dairy margarine (such as Fleischmann's®), frozen
1 large egg yolk, cold
1 teaspoon cold water
1 egg white whisked with 1 teaspoon water, for glazing

Chocolate Creem Filling
1/3 cup plus 1 tablespoon dairy-case soymilk (such as Silk®)
2-4 tablespoons sugar
6 ounces semisweet non-dairy chocolate, finely chopped (see page 15, for brands)
2 tablespoons oil
1 eight-ounce carton Richwhip®, thawed overnight
2 teaspoons vanilla extract

Topping
1/2 carton Richwhip®, thawed overnight

Tips

The tart shell can be made 8 hours ahead of filling. Store it, uncovered, at room temperature.

Garnish (optional)
1 - 3 ounces non-dairy chocolate, shaved
1/2 - 1-1/2 teaspoons canola oil
Chocolate curls or shavings
1/2 pint fresh raspberries, washed and patted dry

1. Preheat the oven to 375 degrees F. Lightly grease an 8-inch tart pan. For the crust, mix the flour, sugar and salt in a food processor. Pulse to mix the ingredients together. Cut the margarine into 1/4-inch cubes and add to the processor. Pulse on and off, until the mixture looks like coarse meal. In a small bowl, whisk together the egg yolk and water. Add to the processor and pulse for 10 - 20 seconds, until the dough starts to come together. Turn the dough out onto a piece of plastic wrap and press it into a ball.

2. To press the dough into the pan, start with gumball-sized lumps of dough. Squeeze the dough between your fingers until it is a scant 1/8-inch thick, dusting your fingers with flour if the dough is sticking to them. Place the flattened dough in the pan. Repeat with the remaining dough, piecing everything together to make a solid crust. To trim the edges, run a rolling pin over the top of the pan. Press the edges up slightly to thin them out and to make the edges a little higher than the pan. Prick the bottom of the dough in several places with a fork. Freeze the tart for 15 minutes or until firm to the touch. Press nonstick

If you want to freeze the filled tart, brush the tart shell with the melted chocolate-oil mixture. Refrigerate to set it, fill with the mousse and then freeze the tart. Defrost in the refrigerator overnight. Add the toppings and decoration after the tart has been defrosted.

To garnish, use a ratio of 1 ounce chocolate to 1/2 teaspoon of oil. In a microwave-safe bowl, microwave the chocolate and oil, on medium, just until melted and smooth. If just drizzling a little over the top of the tart, use 1 ounce. If you want to decorate the platter or individual plates, you will need the larger quantity of chocolate. A simpler decoration would be a sprinkling of shaved chocolate. Garnish with fresh raspberries.

aluminum foil snugly on top of the dough with the nonstick side down. Fill the foil with pie weights or beans. **Bake for 15 minutes**, remove the foil and beans and **bake 5 - 10 minutes** more, until the crust looks dry and nicely browned, brushing the pastry with the egg white glaze during the last minute of baking. Cool on a wire rack.

3. For the filling, combine the soymilk and sugar in a small microwave-safe bowl (using the larger amount of sugar if the chocolate you are using is bitter, or if you just like it sweeter). Microwave on high until hot, about 1 minute. Stir in the chocolate and oil. Swirl to submerge the chocolate, and then heat in 15 second increments, on medium power, until the chocolate is melted. Set aside to cool for 10 - 20 minutes.

4. Pour one container of Richwhip® into a small mixer bowl. Stir in the vanilla. Beat, increasing the speed from low to high, until the topping forms soft peaks.

5. Stir 1/3 of the whipped topping into the chocolate mixture. Fold in the remaining topping. Spoon the chocolate mixture into the tart shell. Cover loosely with foil, and refrigerate the tart for 4 hours or overnight.

6. For the topping, whip 1/2 carton Richwhip® to stiff peaks. Spoon or pipe the cream onto the tart.

Apple Strudel

SERVES 6 - 8
DEFROST THE PHYLLO OVERNIGHT

Phyllo is easy to use, but you must work quickly in order to be successful. Because of the way this strudel is layered, it stays crisper than most, so it can be made up to 8 hours ahead. I use a mix of apples to get the best flavor and texture: Fujis, because they're firm, Granny Smiths for texture and tartness and Golden Delicious for sweetness.

3 non-dairy shortbread, tea biscuit or animal cookies

1-1/3 cups mixed unsalted nuts (such as almonds, walnuts and pistachios)

2-1/2 cups peeled, cored and cubed apples (about 2 large or 1 pound apples), tossed in the juice of 1 lemon

1/4 cup raisins

3 tablespoons sugar or to taste

2 tablespoons sliced almonds

2 tablespoons of walnuts, coarsely chopped

2 tablespoons shelled pistachios (optional), coarsely chopped

2 teaspoons cornstarch

1/2 stick (4 tablespoons) unsalted non-dairy margarine (such as Fleischmann's®), melted

1 tablespoon canola oil

1 package phyllo dough (or 1 roll phyllo if your package contains 2 separate pouches), thawed overnight in the refrigerator and then left at room temperature 2 - 4 hours

Powdered sugar for sprinkling

Once the phyllo has been un-wrapped, it must be used quickly and kept covered with waxed paper, or it will dry out and crumble, like dried leaves. Before opening the box, gather together the apple mixture, cookie mixture, powdered sugar in a sprinkler, parchment paper, waxed paper, cookie sheet, pastry brush and a sharp, nonserrated knife.

1. Preheat the oven to 375 degrees F. with a rack in the middle of the oven.

2. Place the cookies and mixed nuts in a food processor bowl. Process until finely ground. Transfer the mixture to a small bowl.

3. In a large bowl, mix together the apples, raisins, sugar, almonds, walnuts, pistachios and cornstarch.

4. Mix together the melted margarine and the oil.

5. Place a large sheet of waxed paper on your work surface. Remove the phyllo from the box and unfold it onto the waxed paper. To prevent the phyllo from drying out, keep it covered with another sheet of waxed paper whenever you are not removing a leaf of pastry.

6. If you are using phyllo that comes packed two rolls per package, these phyllo sheets may not be quite wide enough to make a nice strudel. You will want to overlap two sheets to make a larger sheet. (If you are able to find phyllo that has sheets that are 12 x 15 inches, you do not need to overlap sheets.). Lay out a large sheet of parchment or waxed paper on your work surface. Remove one sheet of phyllo and set it on the paper with a short side facing you. Brush it with a light coating of the margarine mixture. Place another pastry sheet overlapping the first sheet by 1/2

Strudel can be made up to 8 hours in advance, if left at room temperature, uncovered. Reheat it in a 350 degree F. oven for 15 minutes. Strudel may also be frozen, unbaked, although it's not nearly as delicious as fresh. Let the strudel freeze before wrapping it in foil, and then in a plastic bag. Unwrap the pastry and bake frozen strudel at 350 degrees F. for 30 minutes. Increase the heat to 425 degrees F. and bake for 10 minutes more, or until golden. Let it cool 20 minutes before serving.

inch on the long side. You should now have a sheet that is approximately 16 x 13 inches.

7. Brush the pastry sheet that you have now created, with the margarine mixture, sprinkle with about 2 teaspoons powdered sugar and then broadcast about 2 tablespoons of the cookie and ground nut mixture over the dough. Repeat layering, brushing and sprinkling six more times, with the seventh sheet being brushed with the margarine mixture only.

8. Leaving 3-1/2 inches along the long side facing you and 3/4 inch at each short end, spread the remaining cookie crumbs in a strip, 2-1/2 inches wide.

9. Place the apple mixture on the crumbs, in a mound, 1-1/2 inches high. Fold the 3-1/2-inch un-sprinkled dough over the filling and roll up the pastry, lengthwise, jelly-roll fashion (you can tuck in the ends, but it's not really necessary).

10. Slide the parchment paper onto a baking sheet. Brush margarine over the pastry. Make diagonal cuts, about 1/2 inch deep, every 1-1/4 inches. **Bake for 35-45 minutes** until nicely browned. Set the cookie sheet on a rack to cool for 20 minutes. Serve the strudel slightly warm.

Baklava

SERVES 15 - 30 PEOPLE
DEFROST PHYLLO 2 DAYS AHEAD
MAKE BAKLAVA 1 DAY AHEAD

Baklava is quite simple to make as long as you work fast so that the phyllo doesn't dry out. It does require some prior thought, as the phyllo must be defrosted the night before and the assembled dessert needs to be made at least a day ahead. It's a great dessert for a crowd, as one pan can serve up to 30 people.

Syrup
2-1/4 cups sugar
1-1/4 cups water
2/3 cup honey
1 whole cinnamon stick
3 whole cloves
2 tablespoons Grand Marnier® liqueur or orange juice (for kosher, use Melody®, Triple Sec®, Curacao® or Drambuie®)

Filling
6 cups finely assorted chopped nuts, (unsalted walnuts, almonds and pistachios)
1 tablespoon cinnamon

1 pound frozen phyllo dough, defrosted as directed below

5/8 stick (5 tablespoons) unsalted non-dairy margarine (such as Fleischmann's®)
6 tablespoons oil

1. Defrost the phyllo in the refrigerator overnight and then let it sit at room temperature for 2 - 4 hours.

2. Preheat the oven to 350 degrees F. Gather together: waxed paper, large cutting

Tips

board on which to cut the phyllo, long knife, 8 x 12-inch baking pan (do not use nonstick as you will have to cut the pastry in the pan), pastry brush and a spray bottle filled with water.

3. Combine all of the syrup ingredients in a large pot (the mixture will almost double in volume when it starts to boil) and heat over medium heat to dissolve the sugar. Bring it to a boil over high heat, reduce heat to low and simmer for 10 minutes. Remove it from the heat and reserve. Syrup can be made 1 week ahead and kept refrigerated. Bring it to room temperature before using.

4. For the filling, combine the nuts and cinnamon. In a small microwave-safe bowl, melt together the margarine and oil.

5. Remove the phyllo from the box. Using the pan as a guide, cut the pastry to fit the pan. If your pan is a little wider than the phyllo, alternate leaves of phyllo to make it wide enough. Cover the phyllo with a sheet of waxed paper.

6. Slide one sheet of phyllo into the bottom of the pan. Brush with a light coating of the margarine-oil mixture. Slide another sheet of phyllo on top of the first. Brush again, and repeat this process until there are 15 sheets of phyllo in the bottom of the pan. If there are rips, alternate sheets so that ripped spots are covered by the next sheet.

The baklava may be stored, covered with foil, at room temperature for up to 1 week.

Baklava can be frozen, baked or unbaked. Defrost baked baklava at room temperature. Bake frozen, un-baked baklava for 1 hour at 350 degrees F., and 45 minutes more at 325 degrees F., or until brown.

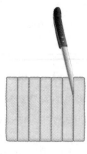

Cut baklava into 1-1/2-inch strips.

Make a diagonal cut through the center and then make parallel cuts every 1-1/4 inches.

7. Spoon on 1-1/2 cups of the nut mixture. Layer on 6 sheets of pastry, brushing each sheet with the margarine-oil mixture. Spoon on another 1-1/2 cups nuts. Layer on another 6 sheets, as above. Spoon on the remaining nuts.

8. Layer on the last 15 sheets of phyllo, brushing all of the sheets, except the top sheet. Cut the phyllo into strips at 1-1/2 inch intervals. Make a diagonal cut through the center and then make parallel cuts every 1-1/4 inches until the whole thing is cut into diamond-shaped pieces (see sidebar drawing). Spray the top of the baklava with water.

9. **Bake 1 hour** or more, until golden.

10. Remove the baklava from the oven. Take the cinnamon stick and cloves out of the syrup and immediately pour the room temperature syrup over the baklava. Let it stand at room temperature at least over-night before serving.

Caramel Pear Phyllo Cups

SERVES 8
DEFROST PHYLLO 1 DAY AHEAD

10 sheets thawed phyllo dough, directions follow

1/3 stick (3 tablespoons) unsalted non-dairy margarine (such as Fleischmann's®)
4 teaspoons oil

1-1/2 cups pecan pieces or halves
1/2 cup sugar
3/4 teaspoon cinnamon

Spiced Poached Pears
3 medium Bosc pears, very firm
1 medium lemon
2 cups sugar
6 cups water
1/2 stick cinnamon
A few grinds of fresh nutmeg
3 whole cloves

Caramel Pear Filling
2-1/2 cups reserved caramel pear syrup
1/4 cup Silk® soy creamer or non-dairy creamer
2 tablespoons thawed Richwhip® (reserve remainder of container)

Combining the fabulous flavors of flaky pastry, caramel, poached pears and chocolate, this is one of my most elegant creations. All of the components can be made ahead and the finished dessert assembled in just a few minutes. For a special event when you want to outdo yourself, this is the dessert to choose.

Defrosting the Phyllo:

If you have a box of phyllo that has two separate packages within the box, remove one package, and place it in the refrigerator overnight. Freeze the other package for use another time. In the morning remove the package of phyllo from the refrigerator and let it stand at room temperature (unopened) for 2 - 4 hours.

For assembly
reserved Richwhip®
3 tablespoons chopped pecans, toasted until fragrant (about 2 minutes in a toaster oven)

Garnish (optional)
3 ounces non-dairy semisweet chocolate, shaved (see page 15, for brands)
1-1/2 teaspoons oil
1/2 pint raspberries, washed and patted dry

1. Preheat the oven to 375 degrees F. To make the tarts you will need eight 3-1/2-inch brioche tins or a regular size muffin pan. I like the brioche tins because you can compress the dough into the wide flutes giving the pastry a harder, cookie-like texture. If using the muffin pan, the dough will get pressed onto the backsides of the muffin cups, so you will want to thoroughly wash and dry that side. Spray the brioche tins or the backs of the muffin cups with cooking spray and set aside. Gather all supplies needed - pastry brush, waxed paper, cutting board, small knife and a round 4-inch cookie cutter.

2. In a covered container, microwave the margarine and oil together, on high, for 30 – 60 seconds.

3. Place the pecans, sugar and cinnamon in a food processor. Pulse until the nuts are finely ground. Pour the nut mixture into a bowl and set beside the cutting board.

Tips

When working with the phyllo, always keep the unused sheets covered with waxed paper. If you do not do this, the pastry will crumble, like dried leaves.

4. When ready to make the pastries, unroll the phyllo, leaving it on the waxed paper that it comes in. Cover the stack of phyllo leaves with a sheet of waxed paper.

5. Pick up one sheet of phyllo and slide it onto a work surface on which you can cut. Brush a light, even coat of the margarine mixture over the pastry, making sure to brush the edges of the phyllo. Sprinkle about 2 tablespoons of the pecan mixture over the dough. Slide on another sheet of dough, brush with margarine mixture, and sprinkle, as above. Repeat until you have placed the fifth leaf of pastry on top of the stack. Do not brush or sprinkle this layer.

6. Set the cookie cutter onto the stack of phyllo and cut down into the dough. Run a knife around the cutter using a chopping motion with the knife, rather than a smooth stroke. Cut out three more circles. Cover the uncut stack of phyllo while you shape the tarts. If using the brioche tins, lift up a circle with a spatula and then set it into the tin. Press the dough firmly into the flutes. If using the muffin tin, press a dough circle onto the back of one of the muffin cups. Press the sides of the dough firmly around the muffin form. Repeat with the remaining three circles. Brush the shaped shells with the margarine mixture. Cover the tin with waxed paper as you prepare the next batch of dough using the same method. You will have 8 completed pastry cups.

The pastry shells can be made up to 3 days in advance and stored in a covered container. Re-crisp by heating at 200 degrees F. for 5 minutes. Freeze pastry shells for up to 3 months. They can be used directly from the freezer.

Store the pears, covered, in the refrigerator for up to 2 days.

The caramel sauce can also be prepared 2 days in advance. Store it in the refrigerator. Stir the sauce before serving and use it cold or at room temperature. Do not reheat the sauce, as the Richwhip will curdle.

7. **Bake for 8 - 12 minutes** until the phyllo is nicely browned and the bottoms are firm. Cool for 5 minutes. To get the pastry out of the brioche tin, turn it upside down and gently squeeze the sides. Let them cool completely on a cooling rack.

8. For the spiced pears, peel the pears, place in a bowl and squeeze the lemon over them. Combine the sugar and water in a large pot. Set it over medium heat and cook until the sugar dissolves. Add the cinnamon, nutmeg, cloves and the drained pears. Simmer the pears for 20 - 30 minutes until tender, stirring occasionally to make sure that the pears are turned and cooking evenly. Remove the pears to a storage container. Reserve 2 cups of pear syrup and pour the remaining liquid over the pears. Set the pears aside to cool. The pears may be stored in the refrigerator for up to 2 days.

9. To make the Caramel Pear Sauce, place the reserved syrup in a medium, shiny saucepan (if you use a dark pot you won't be able to tell when the caramel is the right color). Boil over medium-high heat and cook until it turns golden brown (about 15 - 25 minutes). Do not stir. (You may swirl the pan as the liquid starts to get brown to better assess its progress.) Turn off the heat, tip the pan away from you and pour in the creamer. Stir the mixture until smooth. If necessary, you can put the pot on a low flame to assist in melting the caramel. Remove the pan from the heat and let the syrup cool. Stir in the

Preparation Schedule

up to 3 months in advance:
Make & freeze pastry shells

up to 2 days in advance:
Make and refrigerate
pears and caramel sauce

up to 4 hours in advance:
Whip Richwhip, and refrigerate
Chop pears (leave pears in their
syrup)
Chop nuts
Chop chocolate and combine
with oil

1 hour before serving
Remove caramel sauce from
refrigerator

Just before serving:
Melt chocolate, pat pears dry and
mix into filling, assemble desserts

Richwhip.

10. To assemble, whip the reserved Richwhip until stiff peaks form. Stir the caramel sauce and then add 1 - 3 tablespoons into the whipped Richwhip (to taste). Reserve the remainder of the caramel. Pat the pears dry and then cut and core them. Cut 1-1/2 pears into small cubes and stir these into the Richwhip mixture (you have an extra pear, just in case there are any bad spots in the pear or if you like more pear and less creem). Stir in the pecans. From the remaining pears, cut 1/16-inch slices from each side and roll these up to make little flowers that can top the filling.

11. For the garnish, place the chocolate and oil in a microwave-safe bowl. Microwave on medium, for 1 minute. Stir the chocolate and if not completely melted, microwave for another 30 - 60 seconds on medium.

12. Drizzle the chocolate mixture onto each plate and set a pastry cup on each. Divide the filling among the pastry cups. Spoon a teaspoon of reserved caramel over each cup. Serve immediately, garnishing the plate with fresh raspberries.

Lemon Curd Phyllo Tartlets

MAKES 24 TARTLETS (SERVES 6 - 8)
DEFROST PHYLLO 1 DAY AHEAD

Lemon Curd is traditionally made without a thickener, but it will not thicken properly when made without butter. Therefore, I have added a tiny bit of cornstarch to the recipe that will actually produce a soft-set custard, much like a traditional lemon curd. If you like lemon curd with a definite tart kick, use the larger amount of lemon juice.

Lemon Curd
3 large egg yolks
1/2 cup sugar
1 teaspoon cornstarch
1/3-1/2 cup fresh lemon juice (about 3 lemons)
3/4 stick (6 tablespoons) unsalted non-dairy stick margarine (such as Fleischmann's®)
1 tablespoon grated lemon zest (the peel without the white membrane)

Phyllo Tartlets
12 sheets thawed phyllo (directions follow)
1/4 stick (2 tablespoons) unsalted non-dairy margarine
1 tablespoon oil
1 cup non-dairy cookie crumbs or finely ground nuts
6 tablespoons powdered sugar

Garnish (optional)
Blueberries, raspberries or strawberries

If you have a box of phyllo that has two separate packages within the box, remove one package and place it in the refrigerator overnight. Freeze the other package for use another time. In the morning remove the package of phyllo from the refrigerator and let it stand at room temperature (un-opened) for 2 - 4 hours.

1. Before preparing the lemon curd, place a medium-mesh strainer over a container or bowl. Set it by the stove. In a medium bowl, whisk the egg yolks until blended. Lightly whisk in the sugar.

2. In a small non-corrosive saucepan (do not use aluminum unless you want green lemon curd), heat the lemon juice, margarine and lemon zest, over medium heat, until the margarine melts. Increase the heat and bring the mixture to a simmer.

3. A drop at a time stir the hot lemon juice into the eggs (this is called tempering and is done so that the eggs do not scramble), stirring constantly with a wooden spoon. As the egg-lemon mixture becomes warm, the hot lemon juice can be added in a steady stream.

4. Return the mixture to the pot and cook over medium-low heat, stirring constantly in a figure eight pattern. Make sure that the spoon stays in contact with the bottom of the pot and that it covers the whole bottom, so that the eggs nearest to the heat do not overcook. Bring the mixture to a simmer and cook for 30 - 60 seconds to thicken the mixture. Strain the curd into the storage container. Loosely cover the custard. Refrigerate until cold and then cover it completely. Lemon curd can be eaten as soon as it is cool, or kept for a week in the refrigerator.

5. Preheat the oven to 375 degrees F. Defrost the dough, overnight (instructions in sidebar). Spray-grease 2 nonstick mini-muffin pans. Gather all supplies needed: pastry brush, waxed paper, cutting board,

When working with the phyllo, always keep the unused sheets covered with waxed paper. If you do not do this, the pastry will crumble, like dried leaves.

small knife, 2-3/4-inch cookie cutter, plastic wrap, powdered sugar shaker or medium-mesh strainer.

6. Place the margarine and oil in a small microwave-safe bowl. Cover and microwave on high for 30 seconds or until the margarine is melted.

7. When ready to make the pastries, unroll the phyllo, leaving it on the waxed paper that it comes in. Cover the stack of phyllo leaves with a sheet of waxed paper.

8. Pick up one sheet of phyllo and slide it onto a work surface on which you can cut. Brush a light, even coat of the margarine mixture over the pastry, making sure to brush the edges of the dough. Sprinkle 2 tablespoons of cookie crumbs or nuts over the pastry. Sprinkle generously with the powdered sugar. Slide on another sheet of dough, brush with the margarine mixture and sprinkle, as above. You can make these mini-phyllo tartlets using 4 - 6 sheets of phyllo. With 4 sheets you will have a crisp delicate pastry. With 6, the tarts will be sturdier, slightly chewy and less likely to crumble if picked up and eaten out of hand. For the first time, you might want to take the middle ground and use 5 sheets of pastry. In any case, you want to layer them as above, by brushing with margarine and sprinkling with cookie crumbs or nuts and then powdered sugar. Do not brush or sprinkle the final layer.

9. Set the cookie cutter onto the stack of phyllo and cut out a circle using a twisting motion with the cookie cutter. Cut out 3 or 4 circles at a time, keeping the

The pastry shells can be made up to 3 days in advance and stored in a covered container, or frozen for 3 months. Those stored at room temperature can be re-crisped by heating at 200 degrees F. for 5 minutes. Frozen pastry shells can be filled directly from the freezer (I prefer using the tartlets frozen).

remaining dough covered while you are working. If any of the circles are not cut through to the bottom, use a small knife to finish the job. Lift up a circle with a spatula and set it into a muffin cup. Press down on the phyllo circle to form it into a firm cup shape. Repeat with 3 remaining circles. Brush the shaped shells with the margarine mixture. Cover the muffin pan with plastic wrap as you prepare the next batch of dough. Continue until you have 24 completed pastry cups.

10. **Bake for 6 - 8 minutes** until the pastry is nicely browned and the bottoms are firm. Cool on a wire rack for 5 minutes. Remove the pastry cups from the pans and let cool completely.

11. Just before serving, fill the tarts with a heaping teaspoonful of filling (I use a tablespoon-size mini-ice cream scoop). For garnish, use berries and/or stiffly whipped Richwhip®. If using berries, you can glaze them using 2 tablespoons jam heated with 1/4 teaspoon water (until just thin enough to spread).

VARIATIONS

Chocolate Creem Tartlets – delete Lemon Curd, and use Chocolate Creem Filling, page 188 (refrigerate the filling for 4 hours before using).

Vanilla Custard Tartlets – delete Lemon Curd, and use Vanilla Custard, page 206.

There is nothing like a freshly baked éclair; crisp on the outside, moist and tender on the inside and filled with a creamy filling that you make to order. The glaze is not the grainy, sweet topping found on most éclairs, but pure, real chocolate mellowed with margarine.

Éclairs

Vanilla Custard (Crème Pâtissière)
3 tablespoons cornstarch
6 tablespoons sugar
6 large egg yolks
2 cups dairy-case soymilk (such as Silk®)
3-inch piece of vanilla bean, split lengthwise with one end still attached
1-2 tablespoons softened, unsalted non-dairy stick margarine (such as Fleischmann's®), optional
1/2 cup thawed Richwhip®, optional

Éclair Dough (Choux Paste)
3/4 cup water
1 stick (8 tablespoons) unsalted non-dairy margarine, cut into 4 pieces
1 teaspoon sugar
1/2 teaspoon salt
1 cup bread flour, fluffed scooped and leveled into a measuring cup
2 large eggs, divided, room temperature
3 large egg whites, room temperature

Chocolate Glaze
5 ounces non-dairy semisweet chocolate, shaved (see page 15, for brands)
1/2 stick (4 tablespoons) unsalted non-dairy margarine, room temperature

Tips

1. For the custard: Place the cornstarch and sugar in a medium saucepan. In a small bowl, whisk together the egg yolks and the soymilk. A little at a time, whisk the soymilk mixture into the cornstarch mixture. Scrape the vanilla bean seeds into the pot and then add the vanilla pod back into the pot. Over medium heat, cook about 7 minutes, stirring constantly, in a figure eight pattern, to make sure that the eggs don't overcook. Cook until the custard thickens and comes to a boil. Strain the custard through a medium-mesh strainer into a storage container. For richer, thicker custard, immediately stir in the softened margarine. Press a piece of nonstick aluminum foil directly onto the surface of the custard. Let the custard stand at room temperature until it cools slightly and then cover it and refrigerate until ready to use. If you prefer a lighter, fluffier custard, just before filling the éclairs, whip the Richwhip® and fold in as much as you like.

2. For the éclair dough: Preheat the oven to 425 degrees F. with racks in the upper and lower thirds of the oven. Lightly grease two baking sheets. Top each with a sheet of kosher parchment paper (such as Reynolds®). If you are not good at estimating size, measure and draw the shapes of the éclairs on the curled side of the paper and then turn it so the markings are face down. For large éclairs, draw an oblong 1-1/4 x 3-1/2 inches. For mini-éclairs draw an oblong 3/4 x 2-1/4 inches.

Tips

The choux paste recipe is a little different than most, because it includes egg whites. Adding egg whites creates a drier, lighter shell. If you prefer the denser, richer type of shell, substitute a whole egg for the whites.

When you add the last egg to get the perfect paste, if you don't add enough egg, the puffs will be a little heavy, but if you add too much egg, they will spread out instead of rising up. It 's a delicate balance that just takes a little practice to get perfect. But don't worry – even "imperfect" homemade éclairs will be better than anything you buy commercially and they'll be dairy-free!

3. Place the water, margarine, sugar and salt into a medium saucepan. Cook over medium heat until the margarine melts. Increase the heat to high and bring the mixture to a full-rolling boil. Remove from the burner. Add the flour all at once and stir vigorously to incorporate the flour. Return the pot to a low burner and stir for 1 – 2 minutes until a light film forms on the bottom of the pot (if using a nonstick pot, no film will form, so go by time alone).

4. Transfer the dough to a food processor. Leave the feed tube open to let steam escape and to let the dough cool for a couple of minutes. Process the dough for 15 seconds. Add one egg through the feed tube and immediately process until the egg is incorporated. Add the egg whites in the same manner. Whisk the remaining egg in a small bowl. Add half to the batter and process the dough until the egg is incorporated. The dough is ready if a spoonful falls off of a spoon slowly. If it doesn't fall, add half of the remaining egg and process to blend. Repeat using the remaining egg, if necessary.

5. Spoon the dough into a pastry bag fitted with a 1/2-inch plain tube (the one with the round hole). Hold the bag at a 45 degree angle to the baking sheet and pipe the dough into 1-1/4 x 3-1/2 x 1/2-inch high logs for large éclairs and 3/4 x 2-1/2 x 1/2-inch for mini éclairs. Leave 1-inch

If you eat éclairs often, you might want to buy a special decorating tip that will make filling them easier. Called a Bismarck tip, it has a long needle-like tip that you can insert deep into any pastry. I use it to fill éclairs, cream puffs and jelly dough-nuts.

Cooled éclair shells can be used immediately, refrigerated for up to 8 hours or frozen for up to 3 months. To use frozen éclair shells, defrost them at room temperature. Refrigerated or defrosted éclair shells can be re-crisped in a 350 degree F. oven for 5 minutes (if heating only a few in a toaster-oven, reduce the tempera-ture to 300 degrees F. and watch carefully so the tops don't burn). Let them cool before filling.

Do not freeze filled éclairs.

of space between the éclairs. Using a wet finger, press down on any raised dough tails from the piping tube. **Bake for 20 minutes**. Move the top baking sheet to the lower rack, and the lower baking sheet to the top rack. Reduce the temperature to 350 degrees F. **Bake 15 minutes** more or until the pastries are brown. Remove the baking sheets from the oven. With a knife, make a 1/4-inch slit in the bottom of each éclair to release steam. Return the cookie sheets to the oven, turn off the oven and prop open the door. Let the large éclairs cool in the oven for 30 minutes and the minis for 10 – 15 minutes. Test to see if the éclairs are ready by slitting one open and looking at the interior. You want them to have a dry, crispy exterior, with just a slight bit of moist egginess on the interior.

6. At least 1 hour before serving, make the chocolate glaze. Place the chopped choc-olate and margarine into a microwave-safe container. Microwave on medium for 30 seconds. Stir and then reheat for another 15 seconds or until the chocolate is melted. Dip the éclairs into the melted glaze, refrigerate to set the glaze and then fill the éclairs with the Vanilla Custard. If you need to cut the éclairs in half to fill them, cut them first, glaze the tops, fill the bottoms and sandwich the two together. Refrigerate until serving time, preferably within 3 hours. Serve the éclairs cold.

Pastry • 209

Profiteroles are tiny cream puffs filled with ice cream. The dough is the same as that for éclairs, but because they are filled with ice cream and must be eaten as soon as they are filled, I like to make the shells softer than éclairs. For a sensational dessert, try pistachio ice creem filled profiteroles (suggested by my friend, Lenore Cuyler), or create your own wonderful combination.

Profiteroles with Hot Fudge Sauce

SERVES 5 - 6
AND MAKES 1-3/4 CUPS
HOT FUDGE SAUCE

Hot Fudge Sauce

2/3 cup or Silk® soy creamer non-dairy creamer

9 ounces non-dairy semisweet chocolate, finely chopped

4 tablespoons unsalted non-dairy stick margarine (such as Fleischmann's®), room temperature

1/3 cup light corn syrup

1 teaspoon vanilla extract

1 tablespoon unsweetened cocoa powder, optional

1 recipe Choux Paste, page 206, prepared as directed

1 recipe ice creem

1. Place 1-1/2 inches of water in the bottom of a double boiler. Set it on the stove and bring the water to a simmer. Turn down the heat so that the water just barely stays hot.

Tips

For the profiteroles, it's hard to divide the choux paste recipe in half, so I usually make the whole recipe, using half for profiteroles, and the other half for éclairs or cream puffs (large round shapes that you fill with custard or whipped creem).

Cooled profiterole shells can be used immediately, refrigerated for up to 8 hours or frozen for up to 3 months. To use frozen shells, defrost them at room temperature. Refrigerated or defrosted shells can be recrisped in a 350 degree F. oven for 5 minutes (if heating only a few in a toaster-oven, reduce the temperature to 300 degrees F. and watch carefully so the tops don't burn). Let them cool before filling.

2. Place the creamer in the top of the double boiler. Cook over medium heat until steaming. Remove from the burner and add the chocolate and margarine. Place the pot over the hot water and heat, stirring occasionally, until the chocolate and margarine are melted.

3. Stir in the corn syrup and the vanilla. If you prefer a slight bitter edge, sift and stir in the cocoa. Let the sauce cool. The sauce may be stored for up to 2 weeks in the refrigerator.

4. Preheat the oven to 425 degrees F. with racks in the upper and lower thirds of the oven. Line two baking sheets with kosher parchment paper (such as Reynolds®).

5. Spoon the choux paste into a pastry bag with a 1/2-inch plain tip. Holding the bag straight up-and-down and about 3/8 inch up from the baking sheet, pipe 20 small mounds about 1-inch x 1/2-inch high. Leave about 1-1/2 inches between each puff.

6. Using a wet finger, push down on any tails that have formed from lifting up the pastry tube at the end of the pipe. **Bake for 20 minutes.** Move the top baking sheet to the lower rack, and the lower baking sheet to the top rack. Reduce the temperature to 350 degrees F. **Bake for another 15 minutes** until browned. Remove the baking sheet from the oven. Using a sharp

knife, make a 1/4-inch slit midway on the side of each profiterole, to release steam. Set aside to cool.

7. Just before serving, reheat the hot fudge sauce so that it is warm and thinned. Strain out any lumps. Cut each profiterole in half. Using a teaspoon or a small scoop, fill the bottom half of each profiterole with the ice creem of your choice, mounding it so it will fill the top half as well. Place the top of the profiterole on the ice creem. Set 3 or 4 profiteroles on each plate and spoon the hot fudge over them, letting it run down onto the plate. Garnish with some fresh berries, if desired.

INDEX